OPTIONS FOR FARMERS

A guide to using options for risk management and hedging

JEFFREY KAPRELIAN

Kapco Futures, Inc.
40W125 Campton Crossings Dr.
Suite B
St. Charles, IL 60175
www.kapcofutures.com

This book is dedicated to you, the producer. Thank you for providing the product and livelihood to feed my family.

PREFACE

My goal for this text is to get you, the producer, acquainted with a variety of option strategies that can help manage market risk. Plain and simple.

After working with thousands of producers I completely understand you're not interested in a three-hundred-page book filled with option theory and repetitive examples. For that reason, I'm going to keep things short and sweet. The examples I give have real foundations in risk management, and aren't there just to fill pages.

Of course, I will have to go over the mechanics of options and the various strategies. I feel it's very important for you to understand how things work under the hood. An educated producer is a better risk manager, no two ways about it.

One thing that I think is unique about this text is the application of option strategies to farm revenue. I've seen plenty of examples, and I'll use them as well, of options relative to price, but never revenue. You pay your bills, feed your family, and grow your legacy with revenue, not price. That is a crucial distinction to make.

CHAPTER 1

WHY OPTIONS

"Here's what I can tell you about starting to learn about options. When you first start, the concepts will be confusing. Take the time to learn, and once you work through the steps and the math it will suddenly click."

Options have grown to be one of the most valuable tools a farmer has in their marketing toolbox. They're not always going to be the right tool to use, but oftentimes you are able to accomplish most any risk management strategy using them. The big draw for options is that you have flexibility. Depending on the strategy, you aren't obligated to sell at a price you've set out to protect. You don't have to deliver physical bushels, which is exceptionally handy when you end up with a short crop. You are able to offer bushels at a higher price and have someone pay you money right now to sell them later just in case they trade that high; and if they don't, you get to keep their money!

The list goes on and on, but the point I'm trying to make is that you are able to have more control over your marketing by using options. There are aspects of options that can become very confusing, but those details are generally beyond the scope of what you need to know to be effective. It seems as if the brokerage industry has gone to great lengths to make options appear more confusing than they are, to force you to rely on their expertise. That isn't the case here. I'm going to pull back the veil and show you how options can be used effectively in your marketing plan. By the time you're done reading this, I don't think there will be any confusion as to what strategy to use, how it works, and what it does to manage your risk.

Here's what I can tell you regarding learning about options. When you first start, the concepts will be confusing. Take the time to study, and once you work through the steps and the math it will suddenly click. I know this from when I first started out and from the reactions clients have had. I promise you, the math is nothing more than addition and subtraction. The mechanics are simple when you go back to the foundation of what options are used for: trading the right (or obligation) to buy or sell futures at a specified price.

Each section will be broken down to include the how, when, and why of the strategy. We first look at how the option makes or loses money by itself. Then we consider how it fits in with your inherent long position in the grain market (I'll explain this later). Finally, we will look at a matrix that details what the strategy means for your revenue.

You'll notice that I go to the word "revenue" over and over in this book. It's truly what we're managing. You don't manage price. Yes, you have price risk. But that price risk is a risk to your revenue. Revenue is a function of three things: price, yield, and your cost of production. Read that sentence again; it is foundational. With that, let's move on to some basic definitions.

CHAPTER 2

GROUNDWORK

"What you need to remember is that when someone buys an option, they believe that whatever event they purchased the option for has a reasonable chance of occurring."

Options on futures are one of the most valuable and misunderstood tools available to grain producers. This section aims to demystify the terminology, the costs and benefits of buying and selling options, and how they can be a valuable tool in your marketing toolbox.

To start, let's go over the basic definition of an option on a futures contract (referred to simply) and the two basic types.

First, an **option** gives the right, but not the obligation, to buy or sell the underlying futures contract at a specified price through a specified period. With that basic definition, we can now define the two types of options: puts and calls.

A **put** gives one the right, but not the obligation, to *sell* the underlying futures contract at a specified price through a specified period.

A **call** gives one the right, but not the obligation, to *buy* the underlying futures contract at a specified price through a specified period.

The specified price is known as the **strike price** and the end of the specified period is known as the **expiration**. If one were to exercise their right to buy or sell the futures contract, they would be **taking assignment** of the option.

To receive the benefit of an option one must obviously pay for it. The price paid is known as the **premium**.

When producers think about options, they usually only think in terms of buying them. Logically, if you can buy an option, someone has to be selling it, right? So, let's look at the differences between buying an option and selling an option (also known as **writing** an option).

	Buying Options	Selling Options
Assignment	Has right to take assignment	Has obligation to assign futures
Premium	Pays premium	Collects premium
Goal	Wants option to appreciate in value	Wants option to depreciate in value
Expiration Value (according to CME study[1])	Has value at expiration 23.5% of the time	76.5% of options expire worthless

What you need to remember is that when someone buys an option, they believe that whatever event they purchased the option for has a reasonable chance of occurring. When someone sells an option, they believe the event has a very low chance of occurring. They generally want the option to expire worthless.

There are two ways for an option buyer to get rid of the contract. The first is to take assignment of the underlying futures contract. The second is to **offset** the option by selling it. This is an area of confusion for a lot of producers who are just

---

[1] CME Group: CME Exercised/Expired Recap for Expired Contract Report. 1999.

starting to use options. The only way to offset a put option you purchased is to sell the put. The only way to offset a call you purchased is to sell the call. You cannot offset a put with a call or vice versa.

CHAPTER 3

START WITH FUTURES

"A futures contract is a contract between two parties to buy or sell a specified commodity of standardized quantity and quality for a price agreed upon today for delivery in the future traded on a futures exchange."

To understand options, you first have to understand futures. After all, an option is a mechanism to buy or sell futures contracts. If you lose sight of this simple statement, you'll have a skewed understanding of how to best use options as an instrument for risk management.

To start, we're going to go basic... really basic. A futures contract is a contract between two parties to buy or sell a specified commodity of standardized quantity and quality for a price agreed upon today for delivery in the future traded on a futures exchange.

That's a lot to take in at once, and surely many will have to read that at least a few times to gain a solid understanding of the meaning. Let's break it down in sections.

Two parties

Of course, in any contract there are at least two parties. With a futures contract, someone is buying (bidding) and someone is selling (offering). In your case, a farmer hedging downside price exposure, you will sell to another hedger or speculator who is buying. We don't know the motives behind why the other party is buying, and for our purposes at this point they aren't important.

Specified commodity of standardized quantity and quality

It is the standardization of a futures contract that distinguishes it from a forward contract or any other pricing mechanism. Forward contracts can be set for any number of bushels and for any grade. Futures contracts are traded with a specific quantity and quality. These details, among others, are known as the "contract specifications" and are readily available on each exchange's website.

Corn, soybean, and wheat futures are all traded with a contract size of 5,000 bushels. There are also mini contracts with a quantity set at 1,000 bushels.

Quality, or deliverable grades, is also standardized. All of the contract specifications can be found in the appendix section of this book. It should be noted that, like at your local elevator, there are premiums and discounts on other acceptable grades.

Price agreed upon today

Quite simply, price is price. It is often difficult to think about the price of a futures contract as the price for a forward delivery, because the instant your order is filled and price moves, you are making or losing real money.

Delivery in the future

Futures contracts are traded based on delivery months. The delivery months with most agricultural futures correspond to the crop's production cycle. Delivery dates are set by the exchange and occur in the various delivery months.

This information will be covered in greater depth in the appendix, but the "new crop" month for corn is December, soybeans in November, and wheat in July.

On a futures exchange

Futures contracts are traded on an exchange. The exchange is the intermediary between the two parties and regulates the transaction. Most transactions of agricultural commodities occur at The CME Group, specifically the Chicago Board of Trade. The CME Group consists of The Chicago Mercantile Exchange (CME), Chicago Board of Trade (CBOT), New York Mercantile Exchange (NYMEX), Commodity Exchange, Inc. (COMEX), and The Kansas City Board of Trade (KCBT).

A majority of futures contracts are traded electronically through the exchange. A dwindling number of transactions are cleared through open outcry, also known as the trading floor.

The leading exchange for the "soft commodities" cotton, cocoa, sugar, coffee, and orange juice is The Intercontinental Exchange (ICE).

CHAPTER 4

HEDGING WITH FUTURES

"Equally offsetting price movement sounds great, but there are additional risks to consider."

The Short Hedge

The short futures hedge is the most basic mechanism farmers can use to offset price risk in the markets. Farmers inherently have a "cash long" position simply by being a producer and having something to sell. You essentially own something that can, and likely will, change in value.

If you produce 100,000 bushels of corn and the price of corn goes up 50 cents, you've made $50,000! Great, right? Unhedged, what happens if the price of corn goes down 50 cents? The exact opposite, of course; you would lose $50,000.

What can a farmer do to mitigate this risk? The answer is to use the short futures hedge.

The idea behind the short hedge is to sell futures contracts (shorting) equal to the number of bushels you are inherently long in order to offset the price changes. With the above example of producing 100,000 bushels of corn, a farmer would sell 20 contracts (100,000 bushels) of corn futures in the market. If price goes down the futures profit offsetting the losses in the cash market. If price goes up your cash position gains but the futures lose.

Let's look at an example:

	Cash	Futures
Today (May)	Cash corn is $5.00/bushel	Sell December corn futures at $5.00/bushel
October	Sell cash corn at $4.50/bushel	Buy December corn futures at $4.50/bushel
Change	$0.50 loss	$0.50 gain (before fees and commissions)

At harvest we'd sell the cash corn at $4.50 ($0.50 less than in May).

We gained $0.50 on the futures position, yielding a net sale price of $5.00 ($4.50 + $0.50) before any fees and commissions.

As you can see, the short hedge essentially lets you lock in a price.

The Long Hedge

As we saw with the drought in 2012, grain farmers aren't the only ones who need to protect against price risks. The high prices we saw then were a very tough pill to swallow for livestock producers, or realistically anyone who was an end user. Just as grain and oilseed producers can sell futures to protect against falling prices, end users can buy futures to protect against rising prices.

Let's go back to the same example we used with the short hedge but change things around a bit. Suppose a hog feeder needs to buy 100,000 bushels of corn and wants to lock in a price using the futures market. If on May 1 the price of corn is $5.00, he would buy 20 contracts (5,000 bushels x 20 contracts = 100,000 bushels) of corn futures. Suppose the price of corn then goes up $1.00/bushel by October. Because this feeder was hedged, he has now made $1.00/bushel in the futures market before fees and commissions.

	Cash	Futures
Today (May)	Cash corn is $5.00/bushel	Buy December corn futures at $5.00/bushel
October	Buy cash corn at $6.00/bushel	Sell December corn futures at $6.00/bushel
Change	$1.00 loss	$1.00 gain (before fees and commissions)

So, at the time of purchase the feeder essentially lost $1.00 in cash because price rose by the time he purchased. Meanwhile his futures position increased in value by $1.00 offsetting the cash loss.

Now that we've seen examples of the long and short hedges when price moves work against cash, but for futures we should take some time to look at an example where futures lose but cash gains.

Going back to the short hedge, let's assume the same prices, but instead of the price of corn falling $0.50/bushel we will assume it goes up $0.50.

	Cash	Futures
Today (May)	Cash corn is $5.00/bushel	Sell December corn futures at $5.00/bushel
October	Sell cash corn at $5.50/bushel	Buy December corn futures at $5.50/bushel
Change	$0.50 gain	$0.50 loss (before fees and commissions)

At harvest we'd sell the cash corn at $5.50 ($0.50 more than in May).

We lost $0.50 on the futures position, yielding a net sale price of $5.00 ($5.50 - $0.50) less any fees and commissions.

To sum all of this up, a position in the futures market opposite to that in the cash market is meant to cancel out the effects of price movement in said cash market. Producers of commodities have long exposure in the cash market, so they sell futures contracts. Users of commodities have short exposure, so they buy futures contracts.

Risks of hedging with futures

Equally offsetting price movement sounds great, but there are additional risks to consider. The most obvious is basis risk. Basis risk is the exposure you have to fluctuations in basis that can't be hedged. We can keep things simple here.

If you have a hedge on using futures contracts and basis weakens, you will be worse off by the amount basis changed. It's a fancy way of saying we can lock in the futures price, but you're on your own with basis. Of course, you can lock in basis contracts at your elevator, which is essentially hedging the basis risk.

Interest rate exposure is something to consider if you're a large producer and are financing your margin requirement with a variable rate line of credit. If the market starts working against your hedges and you are required to meet margin calls, the cost of that money could increase.

Liquidity risk is the risk of not being able to enter or exit a position due to a lack of liquidity, or interest in that market. This generally isn't an issue in corn or soybean futures, but in less-traded contracts like oats or rice, there may be times when you're unable to execute the full quantity of your trade near the market or at a price that is further than you expect from the price at which you offset your cash position. Options on less-liquid markets, or even those that are deep in or out of the money (more on this later) in liquid markets oftentimes experience a lack of liquidity.

CHAPTER 5

BUYING PUTS

"In essence, buying a put is buying insurance against lower prices."

Buying puts is the most basic option strategy a grain producer can employ, and oftentimes serves as the foundation for the more advanced strategies we'll later define. For this reason, we'll spend more time on this than anything to ensure you have a complete grasp of this foundational strategy.

Again, puts give the option-holder the right, but not the obligation, to sell futures. In basic terms, this means you are buying protection from a downward movement in price while still maintaining the ability to receive higher prices. If the option expires worthless and you lose the entirety of the premium paid, it means the market has moved higher than the price you were willing to protect. Your net selling price, therefore, is the price of the underlying futures contract less what you paid in premium.

Essentially, a put sets a floor while letting you participate in rallies.

Before we get too far into it, let's back up a step and recognize that you as a producer have what's known as an "inherent long" position. Using corn as an example, your crop is already long the market. If the market moves up, the value of your corn increases; if the market goes down, the value decreases.

All of the charts I'll show will be displayed two ways. The first will show the theoretical profit or loss of the option and the second will show each part of the trade and how it determines your final sale price (not including basis). Those latter charts will show your inherent long position in the market, the legs of the option strategy, and your final sale price. I was originally introduced to the all-encompassing charts I'll show through former CBOE instructor Jim Bittman's 2001 book, *Trading and Hedging with Agricultural Futures and Options.*

So why would you buy a put? The simple answer is because the market is at a price you'd like to protect. You're able to do this without fully committing to that price because of the ability to participate in rallies. In essence, buying a put is buying insurance against lower prices. You pay a premium to be paid back when something bad happens (the market moves lower).

While in reality most people buy puts simply because they think the market will go down, they should be buying them to set a floor under the market that significantly reduces your revenue's exposure to lower prices. That's not always possible, but it is the correct way to use put options.

In this book I repeat the mantra that "your goal should be to manage risk and produce a commodity for revenue." What I'm really saying is that you shouldn't be focusing on price exclusively. That's an easy habit to fall into because price is exciting. It's why you listen to market shows on the radio and TV, and why you buy subscriptions and work with a broker. I can count on one hand how many clients came to me because they were concerned about revenue. Every concept we talk about will be about either reducing risk, protecting revenue, or potentially enhancing it.

With that said, let's look at an example of how a put works in the corn market.

Example: Buy a 450'0 Corn Put for 20'0

This first chart shows the potential profit or loss on a 450'0 put that a producer paid 20'0, including fees and commissions for:

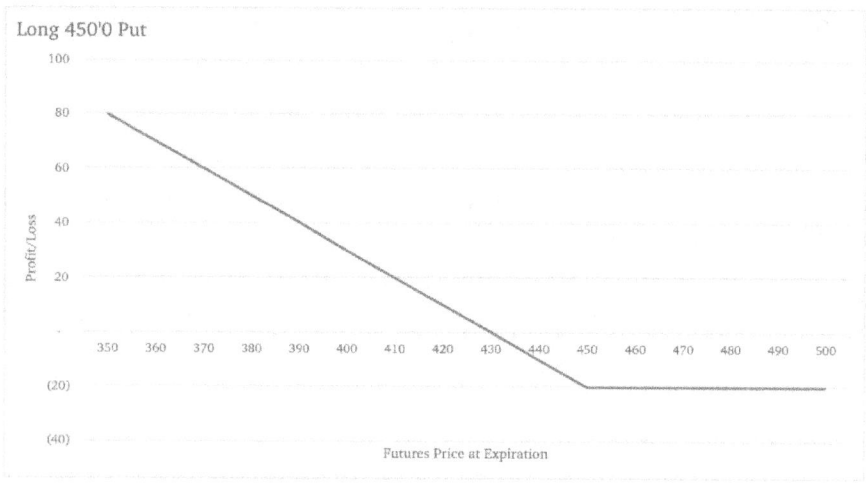

This chart is constructed with the underlying futures price along the horizontal axis (from 350'0 to 500'0) and the profit or loss on the vertical axis. To give you a frame of reference, which will be further explained below, a 350'0 futures price corresponds with a profit of 80'0, while a 500'0 futures price corresponds with a loss of 20'0.

The first thing to note is the downward sloping curve from left to right which then flattens at 450'0. After 450'0 the option is out of the money and becomes worthless at expiration, therefore limiting losses to the premium paid.

17

As prices move lower along the horizontal axis profit (vertical axis) increases. This rise in profit continues on the same slope theoretically until the market reaches zero.

One's breakeven price on a long put is the strike price minus the premium paid; in other words, at expiration profit begins when the put is in the money by at least the premium. So, in the example above where we bought a 450'0 put for 20'0 your breakeven would be 430'0.

Now that you have a basic understanding of how a put makes or loses money, we can look at how they are used in a marketing plan. This is redundant on purpose. It bears repeating! First, and foremost, remember that buying a put allows you to limit downside exposure while maintaining the ability to participate in market rallies. So it can be said that a put is essentially price insurance. That is my preferred way to think of it rather than using it exclusively as a pricing vehicle.

Puts aren't used to make sales; they are used to protect price.

Here is a chart showing a producer's final sale price for bushels protected with the same 450'0 put purchased for 20'0 in the above example:

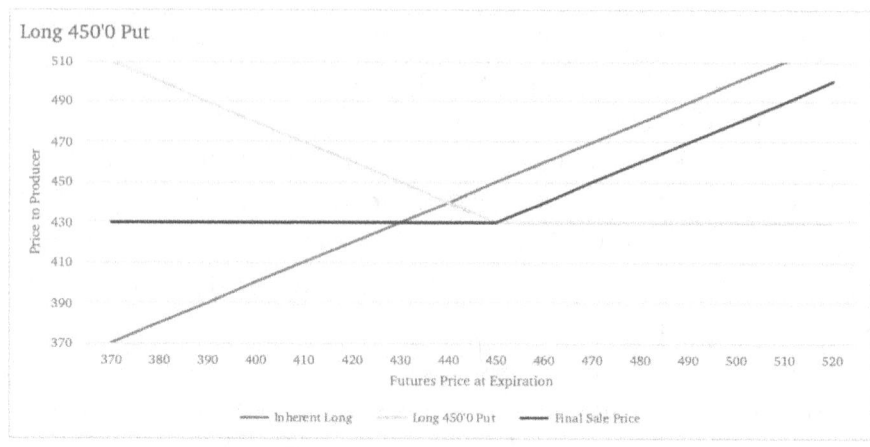

Long 450'0 Put

Let's break this chart down a little, so you can better understand how it is constructed. The horizontal axis shows the futures price at expiration of the options. The vertical axis shows the final sale price to the producer. The light blue line represents a producer's inherent long position in the commodity – corn in this case. The yellow line shows the profit and loss curve of the option, similar to the previous example in this chapter. Finally, the dark blue line represents the final sales price – the price a producer would receive for the commodity, not including basis.

Taking a closer look at the chart, there are a few things to note. First, the difference between the inherent long position the producer has and the final sale price he receives is the amount of premium paid for the option. In this case it is twenty cents.

Second, the final sales price has a level at which the curve stops declining and levels out. This happens at the option's strike price and the final sale price at all points below that futures price equals the strike price minus the premium paid. So even if the market were to fall from 450'0 to 370'0, the producer would still receive 430'0. If the market were to rise from 450'0 to 500'0 the producer would receive 480'0 (500'0 less the 20'0 premium).

Using options to hedge is all about tradeoffs. You can protect any price that trades, but the question becomes at what cost. In the case of buying puts that cost is the premium. You are able to lock in a minimum selling price but you have to give up some money in return. In later chapters we'll discuss how to lessen the premium paid, and what the tradeoffs of doing so include.

In the meantime, let's look at another example using soybeans. Assume the price of soybeans is currently 1100'0. A producer wants to protect against a lower prices and sees 1100'0 puts are currently trading for 50'0 including fees and commissions. He understands this locks in a minimum sales price of 1050'0 and is willing to accept that as a minimum price.

Here is the profit and loss chart for the put position by itself:

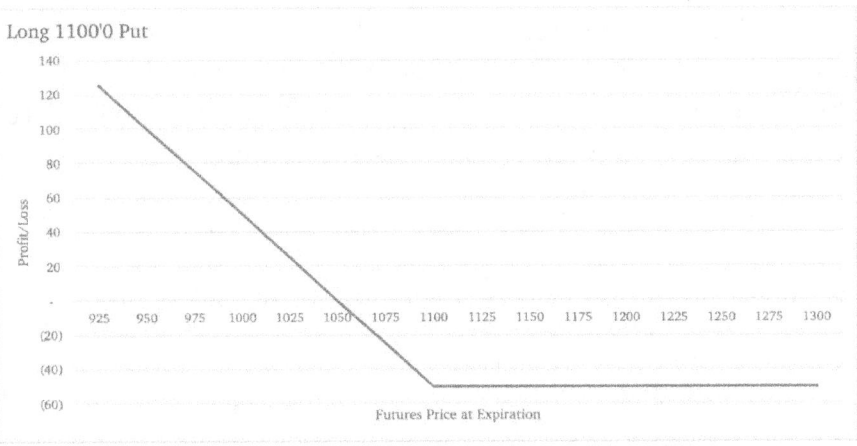

The position breaks even at the strike price minus the premium received (1100'0 − 50'0 = 1050'0). At every futures price at and above the strike price, the option is out of the

20

money and the result is a complete loss of premium. As the market moves below the 1100'0 strike price, the put is in the money by an increasing increment. At 1099'0, the option is one cent in the money and thus the value is one cent. However, because the premium was fifty cents, the position is still a loss (only a 49 cent loss now: 50'0 – 1'0).

So, what does this mean for the producer using the put as a hedge? Well, the minimum selling price for his soybeans is 1050'0, and he is able to capitalize on rallies in price at the futures price minus fifty cents.

By now the advantages of using put options as price protection should be fairly obvious to you. Let's talk about an instance in which they don't work out – when the option expires and the futures price is between your strike price and breakeven. In other words, you bought the ability to capture upside if the market were to have rallied but it saw no upward movement. When that happens, and it often does in a sideways market, on paper you are worse off buying the put than having done nothing.

Consider the above instance in which you bought an 1100'0 soybean put for 50'0. Look at the next chart and notice how if the market were to expire between 1050'0 and 1100'0 you are worse off by the amount of the strike price minus the futures price.

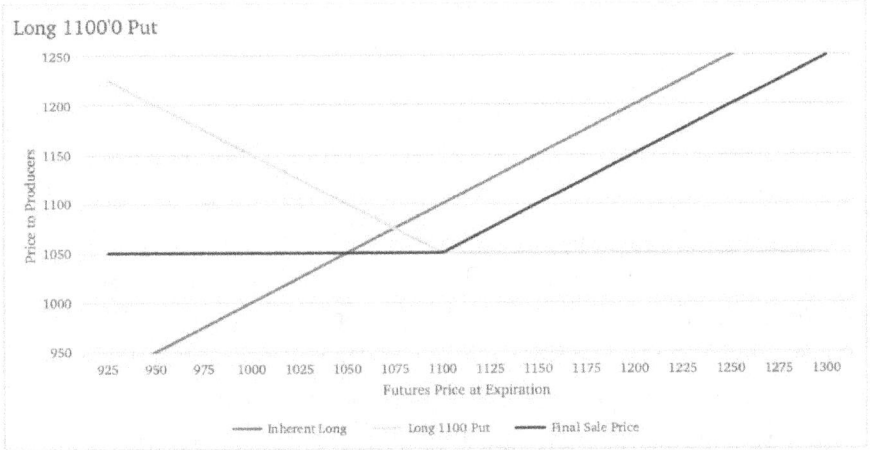

Of course, at every level above the strike price you are worse off by the amount of premium you paid, but that is the cost of doing business when being able to set a floor.

In case you were wondering, the area in which you are better off with the option using the same example is the shaded area in the next chart. It represents any price below your breakeven. That benefit continues to grow from the breakeven down to zero.

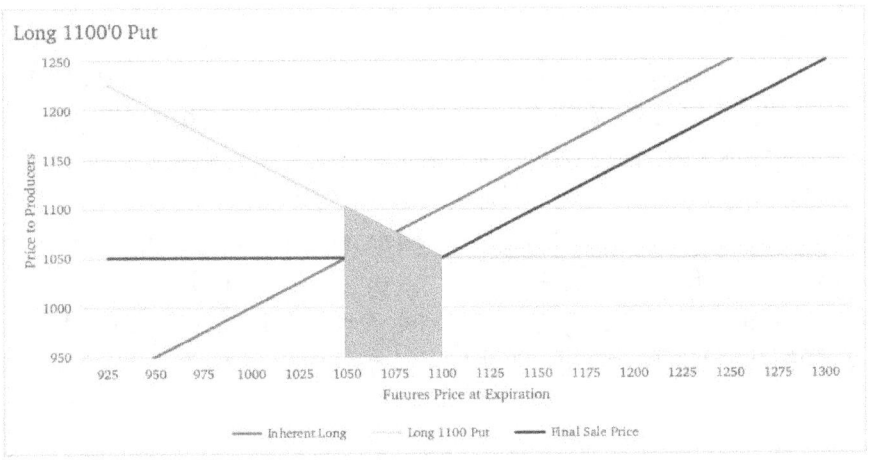

Practical Examples

With the mechanics of how puts work behind us, we can look at some practical examples. And when I say practical, I mean the effect on your bottom line. We do this by entering some hypothetical examples in our revenue management software we developed. This allows us, and users, to test strategies to determine the best approaches to take to maximize revenue while attempting to limit downside as much as possible. It lets you see where you're better off and where you're worse off. This calculator, by the way, is free to use if you're a brokerage client.

And remember, the money you take to the bank is revenue. You don't get paid on price or yield alone.

So, for this example we have to make some assumptions that won't be true for all. However, you can get a copy of the software to test these strategies for your farm. Since I live in Northern Illinois, I'll use some numbers that make sense for my area:

Acres of each crop: 500
Expected yield and APH: 200 for corn and 60 for soybeans
Cost per acre: $700 for corn and $500 for soybeans
This assumes no existing sales.

With that basic information we can derive a matrix that shows revenue per acre at various price and yield combinations. Here, price is on the vertical axis and yield is on the horizontal one:

	-12.5%	-10.0%	-7.5%	-5.0%	-2.5%	Yield	2.5%	5.0%	7.5%	10.0%	12.5%	15.0%	17.5%
	175	180	185	190	195	200	205	210	215	220	225	230	235
4.59	103.25	126.2	149.15	172.1	195.05	218	240.95	263.9	286.85	309.8	332.75	355.7	378.65
4.49	85.75	108.2	130.65	153.1	175.55	198	220.45	242.9	265.35	287.8	310.25	332.7	355.15
4.39	68.25	90.2	112.15	134.1	156.05	178	199.95	221.9	243.85	265.8	287.75	309.7	331.65
4.29	50.75	72.2	93.65	115.1	136.55	158	179.45	200.9	222.35	243.8	265.25	286.7	308.15
4.19	33.25	54.2	75.15	96.1	117.05	138	158.95	179.9	200.85	221.8	242.75	263.7	284.65
4.09	15.75	36.2	56.65	77.1	97.55	118	138.45	158.9	179.35	199.8	220.25	240.7	261.15
3.99	-1.75	18.2	38.15	58.1	78.05	98	117.95	137.9	157.85	177.8	197.75	217.7	237.65
3.89	-19.25	0.2	19.65	39.1	58.55	78	97.45	116.9	136.35	155.8	175.25	194.7	214.15
3.79	-36.75	-17.8	1.15	20.1	39.05	58	76.95	95.9	114.85	133.8	152.75	171.7	190.65
3.69	-54.25	-35.8	-17.35	1.1	19.55	38	56.45	74.9	93.35	111.8	130.25	148.7	167.15
3.59	-71.75	-53.8	-35.85	-17.9	0.05	18	35.95	53.9	71.85	89.8	107.75	125.7	143.65
3.49	-89.25	-71.8	-54.35	-36.9	-19.45	-2	15.45	32.9	50.35	67.8	85.25	102.7	120.15
3.39	-106.75	-89.8	-72.85	-55.9	-38.95	-22	-5.05	11.9	28.85	45.8	62.75	79.7	96.65
3.29	-124.25	-107.8	-91.35	-74.9	-58.45	-42	-25.55	-9.1	7.35	23.8	40.25	56.7	73.15
3.19	-141.75	-125.8	-109.85	-93.9	-77.95	-62	-46.05	-30.1	-14.15	1.8	17.75	33.7	49.65
3.09	-159.25	-143.8	-128.35	-112.9	-97.45	-82	-66.55	-51.1	-35.65	-20.2	-4.75	10.7	26.15
2.99	-176.75	-161.8	-146.85	-131.9	-116.95	-102	-87.05	-72.1	-57.15	-42.2	-27.25	-12.3	2.65
2.89	-194.25	-179.8	-165.35	-150.9	-136.45	-122	-107.55	-93.1	-78.65	-64.2	-49.75	-35.3	-20.85
2.79	-211.75	-197.8	-183.85	-169.9	-155.95	-142	-128.05	-114.1	-100.15	-86.2	-72.25	-58.3	-44.35
2.69	-229.25	-215.8	-202.35	-188.9	-175.45	-162	-148.55	-135.1	-121.65	-108.2	-94.75	-81.3	-67.85
2.59	-246.75	-233.8	-220.85	-207.9	-194.95	-182	-169.05	-156.1	-143.15	-130.2	-117.25	-104.3	-91.35
2.49	-264.25	-251.8	-239.35	-226.9	-214.45	-202	-189.55	-177.1	-164.65	-152.2	-139.75	-127.3	-114.85
2.39	-281.75	-269.8	-257.85	-245.9	-233.95	-222	-210.05	-198.1	-186.15	-174.2	-162.25	-150.3	-138.35
2.29	-299.25	-287.8	-276.35	-264.9	-253.45	-242	-230.55	-219.1	-207.65	-196.2	-184.75	-173.3	-161.85
2.19	-316.75	-305.8	-294.85	-283.9	-272.95	-262	-251.05	-240.1	-229.15	-218.2	-207.25	-196.3	-185.35
2.09	-334.25	-323.8	-313.35	-302.9	-292.45	-282	-271.55	-261.1	-250.65	-240.2	-229.75	-219.3	-208.85

Just to clear up these numbers, corn at 200 bushels per acre combined with a price of $3.69 per bushel would bring $38 per acre in revenue with the assumptions made above.

Not let's add a put to the mix. Assume we cover 100% of our production (200 bpa x 500 acres = 100,000 bushels or 20 contracts) with 380'0 puts with a premium cost of 20'0. Here's what that looks like:

	-12.5%	-10.0%	-7.5%	-5.0%	-2.5%	Yield	2.5%	5.0%	7.5%	10.0%	12.5%	15.0%	17.5%
	175	180	185	190	195	200	205	210	215	220	225	230	235
4.59	63.07	86.02	108.97	131.92	154.87	177.82	200.77	223.72	246.67	269.62	292.57	315.52	338.47
4.49	45.57	68.02	90.47	112.92	135.37	157.82	180.27	202.72	225.17	247.62	270.07	292.52	314.97
4.39	28.07	50.02	71.97	93.92	115.87	137.82	159.77	181.72	203.67	225.62	247.57	269.52	291.47
4.29	10.58	32.03	53.48	74.93	96.38	117.83	139.28	160.73	182.18	203.63	225.08	246.53	267.98
4.19	-6.92	14.03	34.98	55.93	76.88	97.83	118.78	139.73	160.68	181.63	202.58	223.53	244.48
4.09	-24.41	-3.96	16.49	36.94	57.39	77.84	98.29	118.74	139.19	159.64	180.09	200.54	220.99
3.99	-41.91	-21.96	-2.01	17.94	37.89	57.84	77.79	97.74	117.69	137.64	157.59	177.54	197.49
3.89	-59.41	-39.96	-20.51	-1.06	18.39	37.84	57.29	76.74	96.19	115.64	135.09	154.54	173.99
3.79	-74.9	-55.95	-37	-18.05	0.9	19.85	38.8	57.75	76.7	95.65	114.6	133.55	152.5
3.69	-72.4	-53.95	-35.5	-17.05	1.4	19.85	38.3	56.75	75.2	93.65	112.1	130.55	149
3.59	-69.89	-51.94	-33.99	-16.04	1.96	19.86	37.81	55.76	73.71	91.66	109.61	127.56	145.51
3.49	-67.39	-49.44	-32.49	-15.04	2.41	19.86	37.31	54.76	72.21	89.66	107.11	124.56	142.01
3.39	-64.89	-47.94	-30.99	-14.04	2.91	19.86	36.81	53.76	70.71	87.66	104.61	121.56	138.51
3.29	-62.38	-45.93	-29.48	-13.03	3.42	19.87	36.32	52.77	69.22	85.67	102.12	118.57	135.02
3.19	-59.88	-43.93	-27.98	-12.03	3.92	19.87	35.82	51.77	67.72	83.67	99.62	115.57	131.52
3.09	-57.37	-41.92	-26.47	-11.02	4.43	19.88	35.33	50.78	66.23	81.68	97.13	112.58	128.03
2.99	-54.87	-39.92	-24.97	-10.02	4.93	19.88	34.83	49.78	64.73	79.68	94.63	109.58	124.53
2.89	-52.37	-37.92	-23.47	-9.02	5.43	19.88	34.33	48.78	63.23	77.68	92.13	106.58	121.03
2.79	-49.86	-35.91	-21.96	-8.01	5.94	19.89	33.84	47.79	61.74	75.69	89.64	103.59	117.54
2.69	-47.36	-33.91	-20.46	-7.01	6.44	19.89	33.34	46.79	60.24	73.69	87.14	100.59	114.04
2.59	-44.85	-31.9	-18.95	-6	6.95	19.9	32.85	45.8	58.75	71.7	84.65	97.6	110.55
2.49	-42.35	-29.9	-17.45	-5	7.45	19.9	32.35	44.8	57.25	69.7	82.15	94.6	107.05
2.39	-39.85	-27.9	-15.95	-4	7.95	19.9	31.85	43.8	55.75	67.7	79.65	91.6	103.55
2.29	-37.34	-25.89	-14.44	-2.99	8.46	19.91	31.36	42.81	54.26	65.71	77.16	88.61	100.06
2.19	-34.84	-23.89	-12.94	-1.99	8.96	19.91	30.86	41.81	52.76	63.71	74.66	85.61	96.56
2.09	-32.33	-21.88	-11.43	-0.98	9.47	19.92	30.37	40.82	51.27	61.72	72.17	82.62	93.07

You can see that we've practically eliminated price risk while still maintaining upside potential. Because we covered 100% of our expected production, we still have yield risk. You can see here if the farm yields 190 bushels per acre of less at a price of 389'0 or less we are back in the red.

Now remember, we had to pay for the options. So, what's the cost? In other words, where are we worse off?

On the left is the original matrix between 195 and 205 bushels per acre and on the right is the matrix with the puts:

| | -2.5% | Yield | 2.5% | -2.5% | Yield | 2.5% |
	195	200	205	195	200	205
4.59	195.06	218.01	240.96	154.87	177.82	200.77
4.49	175.56	198.01	220.46	135.37	157.82	180.27
4.39	156.06	178.01	199.96	115.87	137.82	159.77
4.29	136.56	158.01	179.46	96.38	117.83	139.28
4.19	117.06	138.01	158.96	76.88	97.83	118.78
4.09	97.56	118.01	138.46	57.39	77.84	98.29
3.99	78.06	98.01	117.96	37.89	57.84	77.79
3.89	58.56	78.01	97.46	18.39	37.84	57.29
3.79	39.06	58.01	76.96	0.9	19.85	38.8
3.69	19.56	38.01	56.46	1.4	19.85	38.3
3.59	0.06	18.01	35.96	1.91	19.86	37.81
3.49	-19.44	-1.99	15.46	2.41	19.86	37.31
3.39	-38.94	-21.99	-5.04	2.91	19.86	36.81
3.29	-58.44	-41.99	-25.54	3.42	19.87	36.32
3.19	-77.94	-61.99	-46.04	3.92	19.87	35.82
3.09	-97.44	-81.99	-66.54	4.43	19.88	35.33
2.99	-116.94	-101.99	-87.04	4.93	19.88	34.83
2.89	-136.44	-121.99	-107.54	5.43	19.88	34.33
2.79	-155.94	-141.99	-128.04	5.94	19.89	33.84
2.69	-175.44	-161.99	-148.54	6.44	19.89	33.34
2.59	-194.94	-181.99	-169.04	6.95	19.9	32.85
2.49	-214.45	-202	-189.55	7.45	19.9	32.35
2.39	-233.95	-222	-210.05	7.95	19.9	31.85
2.29	-253.45	-242	-230.55	8.46	19.91	31.36
2.19	-272.95	-262	-251.05	8.96	19.91	30.86
2.09	-292.45	-282	-271.55	9.47	19.92	30.37

This gives us a really good way of visualizing the obvious: we're worse off spending money to protect downside when the market rallies. From the strike price minus the premium and higher we are worse off. However, puts aren't meant to protect upside, they are meant to protect downside risk. So, at every point below our breakeven we are better off, and this shows you that in terms of revenue – something your banker is sure to understand.

Let's look at another example using soybeans. Beans are a bit more difficult because your revenue is very yield dependent when compared to corn. A two bushel per acre drop in corn is going to cost you less than a value meal at McDonalds. A two bushel drop in soybeans can be $20 plus.

So going back to my hypothetical farm that has 500 acres of soybeans that typically yield 60 bushels per acre at a production cost of $600 an acre we get a matrix that looks like this:

	-12.5%	-10.0%	-7.5%	-5.0%	-2.5%	Yield	2.5%	5.0%	7.5%	10.0%	12.5%	15.0%	17.5%
	53	54	56	57	59	60	62	63	65	66	68	69	71
11.18	86.95	103.72	120.49	137.26	154.03	170.8	187.57	204.34	221.11	237.88	254.65	271.42	288.19
11.08	81.7	98.32	114.94	131.56	148.18	164.8	181.42	198.04	214.66	231.28	247.9	264.52	281.14
10.98	76.45	92.92	109.39	125.86	142.33	158.8	175.27	191.74	208.21	234.68	241.15	257.62	274.09
10.88	71.2	87.52	103.84	120.16	136.48	152.8	169.12	185.44	201.76	218.08	234.4	250.72	267.04
10.78	65.95	82.12	98.29	114.46	130.63	146.8	162.97	179.14	195.31	211.48	227.65	243.82	259.99
10.68	60.7	76.72	92.74	108.76	124.78	140.8	156.82	172.84	188.86	204.88	220.9	236.92	252.94
10.58	55.45	71.32	87.19	103.06	118.93	134.8	150.67	166.54	182.41	198.28	214.15	230.02	245.89
10.48	50.2	65.92	81.64	97.36	113.08	128.8	144.52	160.24	175.96	191.68	207.4	223.12	238.84
10.38	44.95	60.52	76.09	91.66	107.23	122.8	138.37	153.94	169.51	185.08	200.65	216.22	231.79
10.28	39.7	55.12	70.54	85.96	101.38	116.8	132.22	147.64	163.06	178.48	193.9	209.32	224.74
10.18	34.45	49.72	64.99	80.26	95.53	110.8	126.07	141.34	156.61	171.88	187.15	202.42	217.69
10.08	29.2	44.32	59.44	74.56	89.68	104.8	119.92	135.04	150.16	165.28	180.4	195.52	210.64
9.98	23.95	38.92	53.89	68.86	83.83	98.8	113.77	128.74	143.71	158.68	173.65	188.62	203.59
9.88	18.7	33.52	48.34	63.16	77.98	92.8	107.62	122.44	137.26	152.08	166.9	181.72	196.54
9.78	13.45	28.12	42.79	57.46	72.13	86.8	101.47	116.14	130.81	145.48	160.15	174.82	189.49
9.68	8.2	22.72	37.24	51.76	66.28	80.8	95.32	109.84	124.36	138.88	153.4	167.92	182.44
9.58	2.95	17.32	31.69	46.06	60.43	74.8	89.17	103.54	117.91	132.28	146.65	161.02	175.39
9.48	-2.3	11.92	26.14	40.36	54.58	68.8	83.02	97.24	111.46	125.68	139.9	154.12	168.34
9.38	-7.55	6.52	20.59	34.66	48.73	62.8	76.87	90.94	105.01	119.08	133.15	147.22	161.29
9.28	-12.8	1.12	15.04	28.96	42.88	56.8	70.72	84.64	98.56	112.48	126.4	140.32	154.24
9.18	-18.05	-4.28	9.49	23.26	37.03	50.8	64.57	78.34	92.11	105.88	119.65	133.42	147.19
9.08	-23.3	-9.68	3.94	17.56	31.18	44.8	58.42	72.04	85.66	99.28	112.9	126.52	140.14
8.98	-28.55	-15.08	-1.61	11.86	25.33	38.8	52.27	65.74	79.21	92.68	106.15	119.62	133.09
8.88	-33.8	-20.48	-7.15	6.16	19.48	32.8	46.12	59.44	72.76	86.08	99.4	112.72	126.04
8.78	-39.05	-25.88	-12.71	0.46	13.63	26.8	39.97	53.14	66.31	79.48	92.65	105.82	118.99
8.68	-44.3	-31.28	-18.26	-5.24	7.78	20.8	33.82	46.84	59.86	72.88	85.9	98.92	111.94

Admittedly, at $500 an acre there isn't a lot of price risk, but that's the nature of the soybean market at the time of this writing. To regain the scope of this matrix, 60 bushel soybeans at 998'0 yields $98.80 in revenue.

If we add 1000'0 puts that cost 50'0 on 100% of our production, we end up with a matrix that looks like this:

	-12.5%	-10.0%	-7.5%	-5.0%	-2.5%	Yield	2.5%	5.0%	7.5%	10.0%	12.5%	15.0%	17.5%
	53	54	56	57	59	60	62	63	65	66	68	69	71
11.18	56.82	73.59	90.36	107.13	123.9	140.67	157.44	174.21	190.98	207.75	224.52	241.29	258.06
11.08	51.57	68.19	84.81	101.43	118.05	134.67	151.29	167.91	184.53	201.15	217.77	234.39	251.01
10.98	46.32	62.79	79.26	95.73	112.2	128.67	145.14	161.61	178.08	194.55	211.02	227.49	243.96
10.88	41.07	57.39	73.71	90.03	106.35	122.67	138.99	155.31	171.63	187.95	204.27	220.59	236.91
10.78	35.82	51.99	68.16	84.33	100.5	116.67	132.84	149.01	165.18	181.35	197.52	213.69	229.86
10.68	30.57	46.59	62.61	78.63	94.65	110.67	126.69	142.71	158.73	174.75	190.77	206.79	222.81
10.58	25.32	41.19	57.06	72.93	88.8	104.67	120.54	136.41	152.28	168.15	184.02	199.89	215.76
10.48	20.07	35.79	51.51	67.23	82.95	98.67	114.39	130.11	145.83	161.55	177.27	192.99	208.71
10.38	14.83	30.4	45.97	61.54	77.11	92.68	108.25	123.82	139.39	154.96	170.53	186.1	201.67
10.28	9.58	25	40.42	55.84	71.26	86.68	102.1	117.52	132.94	148.36	163.78	179.2	194.62
10.18	4.33	19.6	34.87	50.14	65.41	80.68	95.95	111.22	126.49	141.76	157.03	172.3	187.57
10.08	0.92	14.2	29.32	44.44	59.56	74.68	89.8	104.92	120.04	135.16	150.28	165.4	180.52
9.98	-4.97	10	24.97	39.94	54.91	69.89	84.85	99.82	114.79	129.76	144.73	159.7	174.67
9.88	-4.22	10.6	25.42	40.24	55.06	69.88	84.7	99.52	114.34	129.16	143.98	158.8	173.62
9.78	-3.47	11.2	25.87	40.54	55.21	69.38	84.55	99.22	113.89	128.56	143.23	157.9	172.57
9.68	-2.72	11.8	26.32	40.84	55.36	69.88	84.4	98.92	113.44	127.96	142.48	157	171.52
9.58	-1.96	12.41	26.78	41.15	55.52	69.89	84.26	98.63	113	127.37	141.74	156.11	170.48
9.48	-1.21	13.01	27.23	41.45	55.67	69.89	84.11	98.33	112.55	126.77	140.99	155.21	169.43
9.38	-0.46	13.61	27.68	41.75	55.82	69.89	83.96	98.03	112.1	126.17	140.24	154.31	168.38
9.28	0.29	14.21	28.13	42.05	55.97	69.89	83.81	97.73	111.65	125.57	139.49	153.41	167.33
9.18	1.04	14.81	28.58	42.35	56.12	69.89	83.66	97.43	111.2	124.97	138.74	152.51	166.28
9.08	1.79	15.41	29.03	42.65	56.27	69.89	83.51	97.13	110.75	124.37	137.99	151.61	165.23
8.98	2.54	16.01	29.48	42.95	56.42	69.89	83.36	96.83	110.3	123.77	137.24	150.71	164.18
8.88	3.29	16.61	29.93	43.25	56.57	69.89	83.21	96.53	109.85	123.17	136.49	149.81	163.13
8.78	4.04	17.21	30.38	43.55	56.72	69.89	83.06	96.23	109.4	122.57	135.74	148.91	162.08
8.68	4.8	17.82	30.84	43.86	56.88	69.9	82.92	95.94	108.96	121.98	135	148.02	161.04

The difference is most noticeable at the 60-bushel mark because we ended up buying six contract which protects 30,000 bushels (5,000 bushel contract x 6). This covers 100% of our expected production here. Notice how we end up locking in a minimum $69.89 in revenue at that yield. Of course, as yield goes up, we end up with more revenue, hence the higher prices. As yield falls, we end up with fewer bushels to sell, which means less revenue. The constant is that we were able to eliminate quite a bit of downside price exposure even though we were still profitable at many of the lower prices.

This begs the question: why would a producer spend money on puts when they are already making money? In the previous example using corn we were able to eliminate the risk of losing money at normal yields. There are a lot of ways to answer this, but the most obvious is you want to lock in that ~~price~~ revenue but think the market can still work higher.

Did you catch that? I scratched out "price" and replacing it with "revenue." Assume the producer is comfortable with that level of revenue, and if that's the worst he gets, that's A-OK. In this example, $69.88 an acre is a 14% return on investment (ROI). Every year I run through this matrix with clients and we end up with a number like that. When they hear an ROI like this they usually ask if they should lock it in then hem and haw over it. My response always comes in the form of a statement followed by a question: "You can lock in a 14% ROI doing what you love and I'm hoping to get a 10% return on my investments. Do you need a partner?"

It's a no brainer! If you don't lock in a nice profit when it's given to you, you just did the equivalent of walking down an empty street, looking at a $50 bill on the sidewalk, and kicking it into the sewer.

CHAPTER 6

SELLING CALLS

Selling, or writing, calls is a riskier strategy than buying puts. It allows you to lock in a price, but only if the market continues higher. That means you still have downside exposure. However, what you get in exchange for that is premium. When you buy an option you pay a premium; when you sell an option you receive premium.

Whenever you sell an option the goal is for it to expire worthless. As you'll see in coming chapters, we generally only write calls in combination with some sort of put purchase. The main reason one writes an option is to make the protection you purchase cheaper by collecting some premium.

Just as we broke down the various parts of buying a put, we're going to look at selling a call the same way.

To visually interpret the profit or loss on a short call we use the following chart:

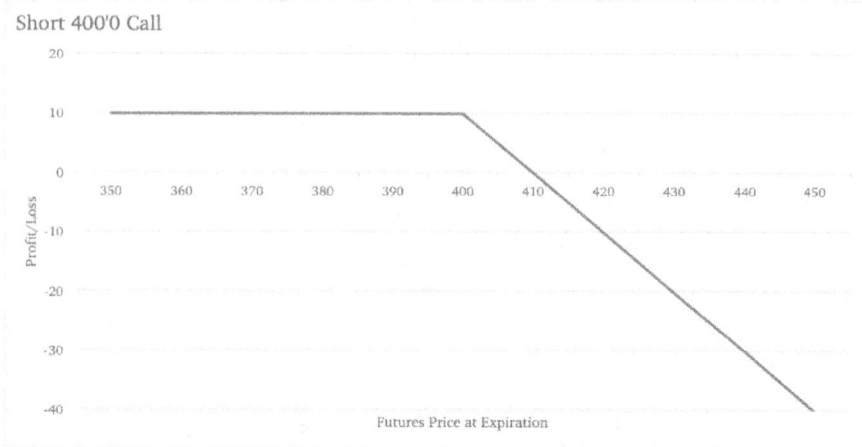

Short 400'0 Call

If we sold the option for a dime, net of fees and commissions, at every level at the strike price or less we have made 10'0 in profit. Our losses are unlimited, however. As the market moves higher the option moves further into the money. That's great news for whoever bought it, but bad for the seller (us in this case). So losses steadily increase as the market moves up.

The breakeven for this trade is the strike price plus the premium received.

400'0 + 10'0 = 410'0

Now we'll look at what this means for you as a producer with the chart on the next page:

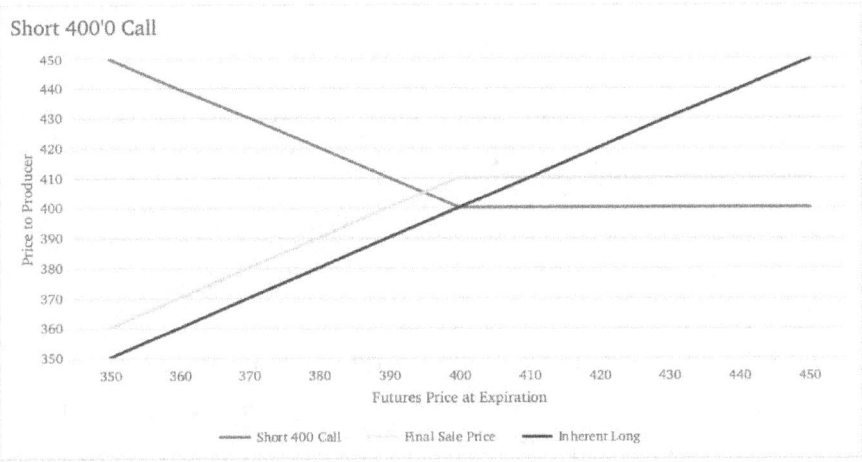

Short 400'0 Call

You can see from the chart that your final sales price is 10'0 better than before at every price up to the strike price plus the premium, at which point they are equal. At that point you are worse off for having the short call than you by whatever the futures price is less the strike price plus the premium.

Here is a table showing this scenario:

Inherent Long	Final Sale Price	Better/Worse Off
350	360	10
360	370	10
370	380	10
380	390	10
390	400	10
400	410	10
410	410	-
420	410	(10)
430	410	(20)
440	410	(30)
450	410	(40)

Let's look at our revenue matrix just as we did with buying puts. We'll make the same assumptions as before:

Acres of each crop: 500

Expected yield and APH: 200 for corn and 60 for soybeans

Cost per acre: $700 for corn and $500 for soybeans

This assumes no existing sales.

For the sake of this example, rather than real life practicality, let's assume we sell 400'0 puts on 100% of our production for 10'0 net of fees and commissions.

Here is what our original matrix looks like (before the short call):

	-12.5%	-10.0%	-7.5%	-5.0%	-2.5%	Yield	2.5%	5.0%	7.5%	10.0%	12.5%	15.0%	17.5%
	175	180	185	190	195	200	205	210	215	220	225	230	235
4.59	103.25	126.2	149.15	172.1	195.05	218	240.95	263.9	286.85	309.8	332.75	355.7	378.65
4.49	85.75	108.2	130.65	153.1	175.55	198	220.45	242.9	265.35	287.8	310.25	332.7	355.15
4.39	68.25	90.2	112.15	134.1	156.05	178	199.95	221.9	243.85	265.8	287.75	309.7	331.65
4.29	50.75	72.2	93.65	115.1	136.55	158	179.45	200.9	222.35	243.8	265.25	286.7	308.15
4.19	33.25	54.2	75.15	96.1	117.05	138	158.95	179.9	200.85	221.8	242.75	263.7	284.65
4.09	15.75	36.2	56.65	77.1	97.55	118	138.45	158.9	179.35	199.8	220.25	240.7	261.15
3.99	-1.75	18.2	38.15	58.1	78.05	98	117.95	137.9	157.85	177.8	197.75	217.7	237.65
3.89	-19.25	0.2	19.65	39.1	58.55	78	97.45	116.9	136.35	155.8	175.25	194.7	214.15
3.79	-36.75	-17.8	1.15	20.1	39.05	58	76.95	95.9	114.85	133.8	152.75	171.7	190.65
3.69	-54.25	-35.8	-17.35	1.1	19.55	38	56.45	74.9	93.35	111.8	130.25	148.7	167.15
3.59	-71.75	-53.8	-35.85	-17.9	0.05	18	35.95	53.9	71.85	89.8	107.75	125.7	143.65
3.49	-89.25	-71.8	-54.35	-36.9	-19.45	-2	15.45	32.9	50.35	67.8	85.25	102.7	120.15
3.39	-106.75	-89.8	-72.85	-55.9	-38.95	-22	-5.05	11.9	28.85	45.8	62.75	79.7	96.65
3.29	-124.25	-107.8	-91.35	-74.9	-58.45	-42	-25.55	-9.1	7.35	23.8	40.25	56.7	73.15
3.19	-141.75	-125.8	-109.85	-93.9	-77.95	-62	-46.05	-30.1	-14.15	1.8	17.75	33.7	49.65
3.09	-159.25	-143.8	-128.35	-112.9	-97.45	-82	-66.55	-51.1	-35.65	-20.2	-4.75	10.7	26.15
2.99	-176.75	-161.8	-146.85	-131.9	-116.95	-102	-87.05	-72.1	-57.15	-42.2	-27.25	-12.3	2.65
2.89	-194.25	-179.8	-165.35	-150.9	-136.45	-122	-107.55	-93.1	-78.05	-64.2	-49.75	-35.3	-20.85
2.79	-211.75	-197.8	-183.85	-169.9	-155.95	-142	-128.05	-114.1	-100.15	-86.2	-72.25	-58.3	-44.35
2.69	-229.25	-215.8	-202.35	-188.9	-175.45	-162	-148.55	-135.1	-121.65	-108.2	-94.75	-81.3	-67.85
2.59	-246.75	-233.8	-220.85	-207.9	-194.95	-182	-169.05	-156.1	-143.15	-130.2	-117.25	-104.3	-91.35
2.49	-264.25	-251.8	-239.35	-226.9	-214.45	-202	-189.55	-177.1	-164.65	-152.2	-139.75	-127.3	-114.85
2.39	-281.75	-269.8	-257.85	-245.9	-233.95	-222	-210.05	-198.1	-186.15	-174.2	-162.25	-150.3	-138.35
2.29	-299.25	-287.8	-278.35	-264.9	-253.45	-242	-230.55	-219.1	-207.65	-196.2	-184.75	-173.3	-161.85
2.19	-316.75	-305.8	-294.85	-283.9	-272.95	-262	-251.05	-240.1	-229.15	-218.2	-207.25	-196.3	-185.35
2.09	-334.25	-323.8	-313.35	-302.9	-292.45	-282	-271.55	-261.1	-250.65	-240.2	-229.75	-219.3	-208.85

And here it is with the option:

Yield	-12.5%	-10.0%	-7.5%	-5.0%	-2.5%	Yield	2.5%	5.0%	7.5%	10.0%	12.5%	15.0%	17.5%
	175	180	185	190	195	200	205	210	215	220	225	230	235
4.59	5.07	28.02	50.97	73.92	96.87	119.82	142.77	165.72	188.67	211.62	234.57	257.52	280.47
4.49	7.57	30.02	52.47	74.92	97.37	119.82	142.27	164.72	187.17	209.62	232.07	254.52	276.97
4.39	10.07	32.02	53.97	75.92	97.87	119.82	141.77	163.72	185.67	207.62	229.57	251.52	273.47
4.29	12.58	34.03	55.48	76.93	98.38	119.83	141.28	162.73	184.18	205.63	227.08	248.53	269.98
4.19	15.08	36.03	56.98	77.93	98.88	119.83	140.78	161.73	182.68	203.63	224.58	245.53	266.48
4.09	17.59	38.04	58.49	78.94	99.39	119.84	140.29	160.74	181.19	201.64	222.09	242.54	262.99
3.99	18.09	38.04	57.99	77.94	97.89	117.84	137.79	157.74	177.69	197.64	217.59	237.54	257.49
3.89	0.59	20.04	39.49	58.94	78.39	97.84	117.29	136.74	156.19	175.64	195.09	214.54	233.99
3.79	16.9	2.05	21	39.95	58.9	77.85	96.8	115.75	134.7	153.65	172.6	191.55	210.5
3.69	34.4	15.95	2.5	20.95	39.4	57.85	76.3	94.75	113.2	131.65	150.1	168.55	187
3.59	51.89	33.94	15.99	1.96	19.91	37.86	55.81	73.76	91.71	109.66	127.61	145.56	163.51
3.49	69.39	51.94	34.49	17.04	0.41	17.86	35.31	52.76	70.21	87.66	105.11	122.56	140.01
3.39	86.89	69.94	52.99	36.04	19.09	2.14	14.81	31.76	48.71	65.66	82.61	99.56	116.51
3.29	104.38	87.93	71.48	55.03	38.58	22.13	5.68	10.77	27.22	43.67	60.12	76.57	93.02
3.19	121.88	105.93	89.98	74.03	58.08	42.13	26.18	10.23	5.72	21.67	37.67	53.57	69.52
3.09	139.37	123.92	108.47	93.02	77.57	62.12	46.67	31.22	15.77	0.32	15.13	30.58	46.03
2.99	156.87	141.92	126.97	112.02	97.07	82.12	67.17	52.22	37.27	22.32	7.37	7.58	22.53
2.89	174.37	159.92	145.47	131.02	116.57	102.12	87.67	73.22	58.77	44.32	29.87	15.42	0.97
2.79	191.96	177.91	163.96	150.01	136.06	122.11	108.16	94.21	80.26	66.31	52.36	38.41	24.46
2.69	209.36	195.91	182.46	169.01	155.56	142.11	128.66	115.21	101.76	88.31	74.86	61.41	47.96
2.59	226.85	213.9	200.95	188	175.05	162.1	149.15	136.2	123.25	110.3	97.35	84.4	71.45
2.49	244.35	231.9	219.45	207	194.55	182.1	169.65	157.2	144.75	132.3	119.85	107.4	94.95
2.39	261.85	249.9	237.95	226	214.05	202.1	190.15	178.2	166.25	154.3	142.35	130.4	118.45
2.29	279.34	267.89	256.44	244.99	233.54	222.09	210.64	199.19	187.74	176.29	164.84	153.39	141.94
2.19	296.84	285.89	274.94	263.99	253.04	242.09	231.14	220.19	209.24	198.29	187.34	176.39	165.44
2.09	314.33	303.88	293.43	282.98	272.53	262.08	251.63	241.18	230.73	220.28	209.83	199.38	188.93

Here you can see the difference at values above 410'0 are worse off, while they are better off below. Again, this is not a viable strategy by itself, but it is important for you to understand the mechanics and effects on revenue short options have before incorporating them in other strategies.

One place where you may be a little better off using these alone is in the soybean market. That is so because soybean options command higher premiums than corn because the price of the contract is higher, and volatility is usually a little higher.

Consider an example where we sell a 1040'0 call on soybeans for 20'0 net of fees and commissions. Here's the original matrix using the assumptions laid out earlier:

	-12.5%	-10.0%	-7.5%	-5.0%	-2.5%	Yield	2.5%	5.0%	7.5%	10.0%	12.5%	15.0%	17.5%
	53	54	56	57	59	60	62	63	65	66	68	69	71
10.7525	64.51	80.64	96.76	112.89	129.02	145.15	161.28	177.41	193.54	209.67	225.79	241.92	258.05
10.6525	59.26	75.24	91.21	107.19	123.17	139.15	155.13	171.11	187.09	203.07	219.04	235.02	251
10.5525	54.01	69.84	85.66	101.49	117.32	133.15	148.98	164.81	180.64	196.47	212.29	228.12	243.95
10.4525	48.76	64.44	80.11	95.79	111.47	127.15	142.83	158.51	174.19	189.87	205.54	221.22	236.9
10.3525	43.51	59.04	74.56	90.09	105.62	121.15	136.68	152.21	167.74	183.27	198.79	214.32	229.85
10.2525	38.26	53.64	69.01	84.39	99.77	115.15	130.53	145.91	161.29	176.67	192.04	207.42	222.8
10.1525	33.01	48.24	63.46	78.69	93.92	109.15	124.38	139.61	154.84	170.07	185.29	200.52	215.75
10.0525	27.76	42.84	57.91	72.99	88.07	103.15	118.23	133.31	148.39	163.47	178.54	193.62	208.7
9.9525	22.51	37.44	52.36	67.29	82.22	97.15	112.08	127.01	141.94	156.87	171.79	186.72	201.65
9.8525	17.26	32.04	46.81	61.59	76.37	91.15	105.93	120.71	135.49	150.27	165.04	179.82	194.6
9.7525	12.01	26.64	41.26	55.89	70.52	85.15	99.78	114.41	129.04	143.67	158.29	172.92	187.55
9.6525	6.76	21.24	35.71	50.19	64.67	79.15	93.63	108.11	122.59	137.07	151.54	166.02	180.5
9.5525	1.51	15.84	30.16	44.49	58.82	73.15	87.48	101.81	116.14	130.47	144.79	159.12	173.45
9.4525	-3.74	10.44	24.61	38.79	52.97	67.15	81.33	95.51	109.69	123.87	138.04	152.22	166.4
9.3525	-8.99	5.04	19.06	33.09	47.12	61.15	75.18	89.21	103.24	117.27	131.29	145.32	159.35
9.2525	-14.24	-0.36	13.51	27.39	41.27	55.15	69.03	82.91	96.79	110.67	124.54	138.42	152.3
9.1525	-19.49	-5.76	7.96	21.69	35.42	49.15	62.88	76.61	90.34	104.07	117.79	131.52	145.25
9.0525	-24.74	-11.16	2.41	15.99	29.57	43.15	56.73	70.31	83.89	97.47	111.04	124.62	138.2
8.9525	-29.99	-16.56	-3.14	10.29	23.72	37.15	50.58	64.01	77.44	90.87	104.29	117.72	131.15
8.8525	-35.24	-21.96	-8.69	4.59	17.87	31.15	44.43	57.71	70.99	84.27	97.54	110.82	124.1
8.7525	-40.49	-27.36	-14.24	-1.11	12.02	25.15	38.28	51.41	64.54	77.67	90.79	103.92	117.05
8.6525	-45.74	-32.76	-19.79	-6.81	6.17	19.15	32.13	45.11	58.09	71.07	84.04	97.02	110
8.5525	-50.99	-38.16	-25.34	-12.51	0.32	13.15	25.98	38.81	51.64	64.47	77.29	90.12	102.95
8.4525	-56.24	-43.56	-30.89	-18.21	-5.53	7.15	19.83	32.51	45.19	57.87	70.54	83.22	95.9
8.3525	-61.49	-48.96	-36.44	-23.91	-11.38	1.15	13.68	26.21	38.74	51.27	63.79	76.32	88.85
8.2525	-66.74	-54.36	-41.89	-29.61	-17.23	-4.85	7.53	19.91	32.29	44.67	57.04	69.42	81.8

Now here it is with the short call:

	-12.5%	-10.0%	-7.5%	-5.0%	-2.5%	Yield	2.5%	5.0%	7.5%	10.0%	12.5%	15.0%	17.5%
	53	54	56	57	59	60	62	63	65	66	68	69	71
10.7525	55.23	71.36	87.48	103.61	119.74	135.87	152	168.13	184.26	200.39	216.51	232.64	248.77
10.6525	55.98	71.96	87.94	103.91	119.89	135.87	151.85	167.83	183.81	199.79	215.77	231.74	247.72
10.5525	56.73	72.56	88.39	104.22	120.04	135.87	151.7	167.53	183.36	199.19	215.02	230.85	246.67
10.4525	57.48	73.16	88.84	104.52	120.2	135.87	151.55	167.23	182.91	198.59	214.27	229.95	245.63
10.3525	55.38	70.91	86.44	101.97	117.5	133.03	148.55	164.08	179.61	195.14	210.67	226.2	241.73
10.2525	50.13	65.51	80.89	96.27	111.65	127.03	142.41	157.78	173.16	188.54	203.92	219.3	234.68
10.1525	44.88	60.11	75.34	90.57	105.8	121.03	136.26	151.49	166.71	181.94	197.17	212.4	227.63
10.0525	39.64	54.71	69.79	84.87	99.95	115.03	130.11	145.19	160.27	175.34	190.42	205.5	220.58
9.9525	34.39	49.32	64.24	79.17	94.1	109.03	123.96	138.89	153.82	168.75	183.67	198.6	213.53
9.8525	29.14	43.92	58.7	73.47	88.25	103.03	117.81	132.59	147.37	162.15	176.93	191.7	206.48
9.7525	23.89	38.52	53.15	67.78	82.4	97.03	111.66	126.29	140.92	155.55	170.18	184.81	199.43
9.6525	18.64	33.12	47.6	62.08	76.56	91.03	105.51	119.99	134.47	148.95	163.43	177.91	192.39
9.5525	13.39	27.72	42.05	56.38	70.71	85.04	99.36	113.69	128.02	142.35	156.68	171.01	185.34
9.4525	8.14	22.32	36.5	50.68	64.86	79.04	93.22	107.39	121.57	135.75	149.93	164.11	178.29
9.3525	2.89	16.92	30.95	44.98	59.01	73.04	87.07	101.1	115.12	129.15	143.18	157.21	171.24
9.2525	-2.35	11.52	25.4	39.28	53.16	67.04	80.92	94.8	108.68	122.55	136.43	150.31	164.19
9.1525	-7.6	6.13	19.85	33.58	47.31	61.04	74.77	88.5	102.23	115.96	129.68	143.41	157.14
9.0525	-12.85	0.73	14.31	27.88	41.46	55.04	68.62	82.2	95.78	109.36	122.94	136.51	150.09
8.9525	-18.1	-4.67	8.76	22.19	35.61	49.04	62.47	75.9	89.33	102.76	116.19	129.62	143.04
8.8525	-23.35	-10.07	3.21	16.49	29.77	43.04	56.32	69.6	82.88	96.16	109.44	122.72	136
8.7525	-28.6	-15.47	-2.34	10.79	23.92	37.04	50.17	63.3	76.43	89.56	102.69	115.82	128.95
8.6525	-33.85	-20.87	-7.89	5.09	18.07	31.05	44.02	57	69.98	82.96	95.94	108.92	121.9
8.5525	-39.1	-26.27	-13.44	-0.61	12.22	25.05	37.88	50.7	63.53	76.36	89.19	102.02	114.85
8.4525	-44.35	-31.67	-18.99	-6.31	6.37	19.05	31.73	44.41	57.08	69.76	82.44	95.12	107.8
8.3525	-49.59	-37.07	-24.54	-12.01	0.52	13.05	25.58	38.11	50.64	63.16	75.69	88.22	100.75
8.2525	-54.84	-42.46	-30.09	-17.71	-5.33	7.05	19.43	31.81	44.19	56.57	68.94	81.32	93.7

At levels above 1060'0 (1040'0 strike plus the 20'0 premium), we are worse off than before. However, at all price levels below we are better off. This strategy could make a lot of sense if your main concern is not showing a loss and the market is at levels that are close to your breakeven. This is so because you are receiving money back which essentially pushes your breakeven down to a lower price level.

It's important to keep in mind that selling options involves an unlimited risk of loss on the position and that it carries a margin requirement. Always consult an experienced broker to determine the appropriateness of a short option strategy.

CHAPTER 6

PROTECTIVE COLLAR

"You'd buy a collar if the market is at a price you're willing to protect but it is just a bit too costly to do so with a straight put."

A very common protection strategy for both hedgers and speculators is a protective collar. That is really just a fancy name for buying a put and selling a call. You've seen how both of those work individually, but this chapter will go on to show how they work together, when to use them, and what it means for your farm's revenue.

As you'll come to see, a protective collar sets a floor while letting you participate in a rally up to a certain price. Essentially, setting a band around the levels of market participation (no downside beyond a point and no upside beyond a point), hence the term "collar." This is accomplished by buying either an at-the-money put or slightly out-of-the-money put and selling an out-of-the-money call. The reason you add the short call to the long put is because it brings the total premium you pay down. Remember, the less premium you pay, the higher your floor you receive. The put sets the floor while the short call regains some premium to cheapen the put you purchased. A "no cost" collar is when the sale of an out-of-the-money call completely offsets the cost of an out-of-the-money put.

Let's start with figuring out why you'd do a collar rather than buy a put or hedge with a futures contract. It can be said that you'd buy a collar if the market is at a price you're willing to protect but it is just a bit too costly to do so with a straight put. You'd buy a collar over a futures hedge or cash sale because you still believe there is more upside in the market.

The first example I want to show you is when the market is at a profitable price that you'd like to lock in but still leave some upside open. Let's look at soybeans and first show the inherent long position you have simply from having the crop. Assume the current market price is $10.00:

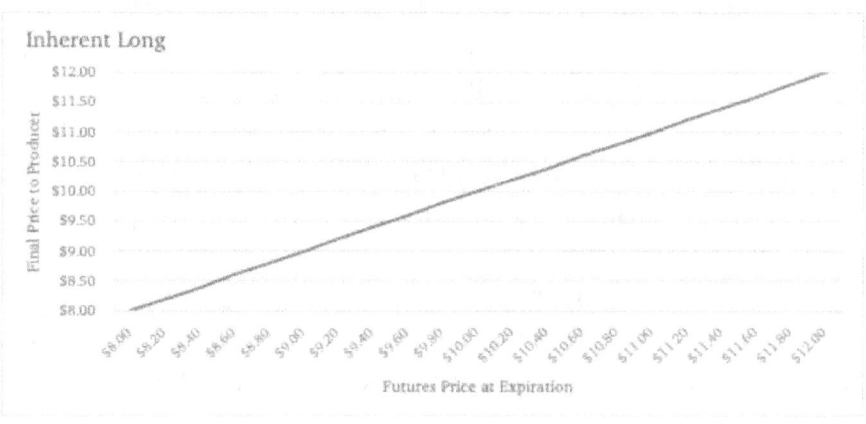

Now let's add in an at-the-money put $10.00 put purchased for $0.50 including fees and commissions:

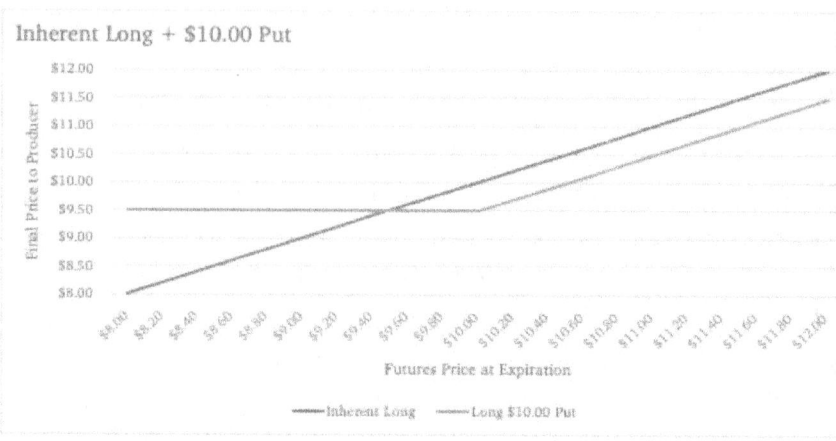

Inherent Long + $10.00 Put

Final Price to Producer

Futures Price at Expiration

——Inherent Long ——Long $10.00 Put

Recall the final futures price to the producer for a put that is in the money is equal to the strike price minus the premium paid minus fees and commissions. So, in this example, all futures prices at expiration that are $10.00 or less yield a final price to the producer of $9.50. If the put expires out of the money (worthless) the final price to the producer is the price at expiration minus the premium paid. As an example, if at expiration the futures price is $10.50 the price to the producer is $10.00 ($10.50 - $0.50).

Now let's add a short call to the equation. Let's assume we can sell an $11.00 call for $0.25. Recall this caps your upside at the strike price plus the premium received ($11.25 in this case).

You can see the final price to the producer is $0.25 greater than the futures price at expiration if the option expires out of the money (worthless). Again, this is because when you sell an option you are paid the premium. If the option expires in the money it limits the final sale price to the producer at the strike price plus the premium received ($11.25).

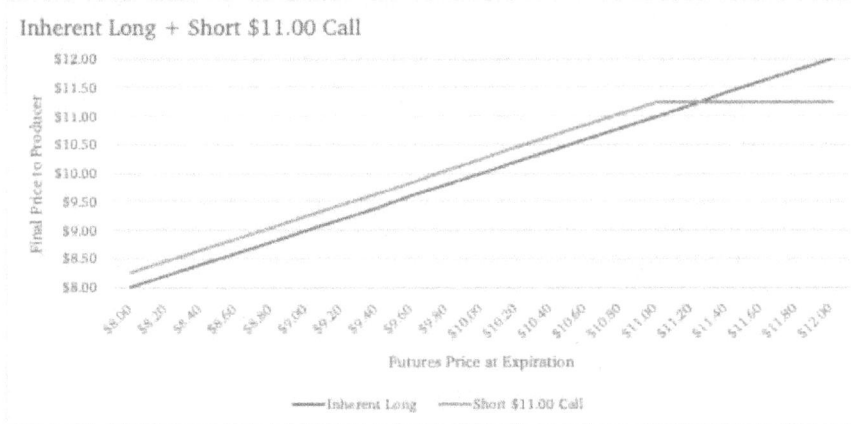

Inherent Long + Short $11.00 Call

When the long put and short call are combined it gives the benefit of the floor from the put plus the premium received from the short call. To continue with the existing numbers, we are buying a $10.00 put for $0.50 and selling an $11.00 call for $0.25.

As you can see on the next page, with the combination of the long put and short call you have both a floor and a ceiling for the final price to the producer. Let's go through the math one final time before we continue analyzing the chart.

Net price paid for the strategy: put premium – call premium + fees and commissions (3 cents, in this example)
$0.50 - $0.25 + $0.03 = $0.28

Floor:
Put strike price – net price paid for the strategy
$10.00 - $0.28 = $9.72

Ceiling:
Call strike price – net price paid for the strategy
$11.00 - $0.28 = $10.72

Looking at that previous chart, the producer is better off when the combination line is higher than the inherent long line on the vertical axis. They are worse off when it is below. Interpreted visually:

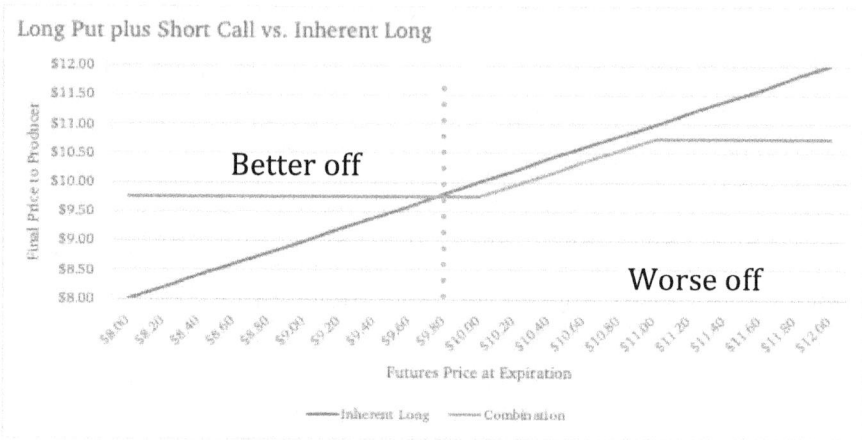

Let's put this into revenue terms. Recall our earlier chart examples that show a matrix with price on the vertical axis and yield on the horizontal axis.

Here's a matrix for a soybean producer with 500 acres of soybeans, a typical yield of 60 bushels per acre, and a cost of $550 per acre:

	-12.5%	-10.0%	-7.5%	-5.0%	-2.5%	Yield	2.5%	5.0%	7.5%	10.0%	12.5%	15.0%	17.5%
	53	54	56	57	59	60	62	63	65	66	68	69	71
11.2875	42.59	59.53	76.46	93.39	110.32	127.25	144.18	161.11	178.04	194.98	211.91	228.84	245.77
11.1875	37.34	54.13	70.91	87.69	104.47	121.25	138.03	154.81	171.59	188.38	205.16	221.94	238.72
11.0875	32.09	48.73	65.36	81.99	98.62	115.25	131.88	148.51	165.14	181.78	198.41	215.04	231.67
10.9875	26.84	43.33	59.81	76.29	92.77	109.25	125.73	142.21	158.69	175.18	191.66	208.14	224.62
10.8875	21.59	37.93	54.26	70.59	86.92	103.25	119.58	135.91	152.24	168.58	184.91	201.24	217.57
10.7875	16.34	32.53	48.71	64.89	81.07	97.25	113.43	129.61	145.79	161.98	178.16	194.34	210.52
10.6875	11.09	27.13	43.16	59.19	75.22	91.25	107.28	123.31	139.34	155.38	171.41	187.44	203.47
10.5875	5.84	21.73	37.61	53.49	69.37	85.25	101.13	117.01	132.89	148.78	164.66	180.54	196.42
10.4875	0.59	16.33	32.06	47.79	63.52	79.25	94.98	110.71	126.44	142.18	157.91	173.64	189.37
10.3875	-4.66	10.93	26.51	42.09	57.67	73.25	88.83	104.41	119.99	135.58	151.16	166.74	182.32
10.2875	-9.91	5.53	20.96	36.39	51.82	67.25	82.68	98.11	113.54	128.98	144.41	159.84	175.27
10.1875	-15.16	0.13	15.41	30.69	45.97	61.25	76.53	91.81	107.09	122.38	137.66	152.94	168.22
10.0875	-20.41	-5.27	9.86	24.99	40.12	55.25	70.38	85.51	100.64	115.78	130.91	146.04	161.17
9.9875	-25.66	-10.67	4.31	19.29	34.27	49.25	64.23	79.21	94.19	109.18	124.16	139.14	154.12
9.8875	-30.91	-16.07	-1.24	13.59	28.42	43.25	58.08	72.91	87.74	102.58	117.41	132.24	147.07
9.7875	-36.16	-21.47	-6.79	7.89	22.57	37.25	51.93	66.61	81.29	95.98	110.66	125.34	140.02
9.6875	-41.41	-26.87	-12.34	2.19	16.72	31.25	45.78	60.31	74.84	89.38	103.91	118.44	132.97
9.5875	-46.66	-32.27	-17.89	-3.51	10.87	25.25	39.63	54.01	68.39	82.78	97.16	111.54	125.92
9.4875	-51.91	-37.67	-23.44	-9.21	5.02	19.25	33.48	47.71	61.94	76.18	90.41	104.64	118.87
9.3875	-57.16	-43.07	-28.99	-14.91	-0.83	13.25	27.33	41.41	55.49	69.58	83.66	97.74	111.82
9.2875	-62.41	-48.47	-34.54	-20.61	-6.68	7.25	21.18	35.11	49.04	62.98	76.91	90.84	104.77
9.1875	-67.66	-53.87	-40.09	-26.31	-12.53	1.25	15.03	28.81	42.59	56.38	70.16	83.94	97.72
9.0875	-72.91	-59.27	-45.64	-32.01	-18.38	-4.75	8.88	22.51	36.14	49.78	63.41	77.04	90.67
8.9875	-78.16	-64.67	-51.19	-37.71	-24.23	-10.75	2.73	16.21	29.69	43.18	56.66	70.14	83.62
8.8875	-83.41	-70.07	-56.74	-43.41	-30.08	-16.75	-3.42	9.91	23.24	36.58	49.91	63.24	76.57
8.7875	-88.66	-75.47	-62.29	-49.11	-35.93	-22.75	-9.57	3.61	16.79	29.98	43.16	56.34	69.52

Red cells indicate losses while green cells indicate profit. This is all in terms of per acre revenue. Now let's add the protective collar in the previous example; buying $10.00 puts and selling $11.00 calls for a net cost of $0.28:

	-12.5%	-10.0%	-7.5%	-5.0%	-2.5%	Yield	2.5%	5.0%	7.5%	10.0%	12.5%	15.0%	17.5%
	53	54	56	57	59	60	62	63	65	66	68	69	71
11.2875	10.07	27	43.94	60.87	77.8	94.73	111.66	128.59	145.52	162.45	179.39	196.32	213.25
11.1875	10.83	27.61	44.39	61.17	77.95	94.73	111.51	128.29	145.08	161.86	178.64	195.42	212.2
11.0875	11.58	28.21	44.84	61.47	78.1	94.73	111.37	128	144.63	161.26	177.89	194.52	211.15
10.9875	11.58	28.06	44.54	61.02	77.51	93.99	110.47	126.95	143.43	159.91	176.39	192.87	209.36
10.8875	6.33	22.66	38.99	55.33	71.66	87.99	104.32	120.65	136.98	153.31	169.64	185.98	202.31
10.7875	1.08	17.27	33.45	49.63	65.81	81.99	98.17	114.35	130.53	146.72	162.9	179.08	195.26
10.6875	-4.16	11.87	27.9	43.93	59.96	75.99	92.02	108.06	124.09	140.12	156.15	172.18	188.21
10.5875	-9.41	6.47	22.35	38.23	54.11	70	85.88	101.76	117.64	133.52	149.4	165.28	181.16
10.4875	-14.66	1.07	16.8	32.54	48.27	64	79.73	95.46	111.19	126.92	142.65	158.39	174.12
10.3875	-19.91	-4.32	11.26	26.84	42.42	58	73.58	89.16	104.74	120.33	135.91	151.49	167.07
10.2875	-25.15	-9.72	5.71	21.14	36.57	52	67.43	82.87	98.3	113.73	129.16	144.59	160.02
10.1875	-30.4	-15.12	0.16	15.44	30.72	46.01	61.29	76.57	91.85	107.13	122.41	137.69	152.97
10.0875	-35.65	-20.52	-5.39	9.75	24.88	40.01	55.14	70.27	85.4	100.53	115.66	130.8	145.93
9.9875	-40.15	-25.16	-10.18	4.8	19.78	34.76	49.74	64.72	79.7	94.69	109.67	124.65	139.63
9.8875	-39.39	-24.56	-9.73	5.1	19.93	34.76	49.59	64.43	79.26	94.09	108.92	123.75	138.58
9.7875	-38.64	-23.96	-9.28	5.4	20.08	34.77	49.45	64.13	78.81	93.49	108.17	122.85	137.53
9.6875	-37.89	-23.36	-8.83	5.71	20.24	34.77	49.3	63.83	78.36	92.89	107.42	121.96	136.49
9.5875	-37.14	-22.75	-8.37	6.01	20.39	34.77	49.15	63.53	77.91	92.29	106.68	121.06	135.44
9.4875	-36.38	-22.15	-7.92	6.31	20.54	34.77	49	63.23	77.47	91.7	105.93	120.16	134.39
9.3875	-35.63	-21.55	-7.47	6.61	20.69	34.77	48.86	62.94	77.02	91.1	105.18	119.26	133.34
9.2875	-34.88	-20.95	-7.02	6.91	20.85	34.78	48.71	62.64	76.57	90.5	104.43	118.36	132.3
9.1875	-34.13	-20.35	-6.56	7.22	21	34.78	48.56	62.34	76.12	89.9	103.69	117.47	131.25
9.0875	-33.37	-19.74	-6.11	7.52	21.15	34.78	48.41	62.04	75.68	89.31	102.94	116.57	130.2
8.9875	-32.62	-19.14	-5.66	7.82	21.3	34.78	48.27	61.75	75.23	88.71	102.19	115.67	129.15
8.8875	-31.87	-18.54	-5.21	8.12	21.46	34.79	48.12	61.45	74.78	88.11	101.44	114.77	128.11
8.7875	-31.12	-17.94	-4.75	8.43	21.61	34.79	47.97	61.15	74.33	87.51	100.7	113.88	127.06

If you compare the two side by side, you see this has eliminated downside price risk on all prices displayed on the matrix down to a yield loss of 7.5% At a normal yield for this producer of 60 bushels per acre they have locked in a minimum $34.76 per acre.

The producer is slightly worse off in revenue terms if the market rallies, since they ultimately had to pay something for the spread and are capping upside at $11.00. As such, this slightly increases price risk at sub-par yields. To easily interpret that notice how the breakeven (green to red) in the furthest left column of 53 bushels per acre moves from $10.38 ¾ to $10.68 ¾ with the option. As with any option, whenever you are able to protect downside it comes at a cost. Whether that is premium cost or opportunity cost there will always be a tradeoff.

No cost collar

A no cost collar works the same way as the previous example. The key difference is rather than buy an at the money put you buy an out of the money put. The idea is the call you sell completely covers the cost of the put, and ideally the fees and commissions as well. Hence the term "no cost."

This is a great strategy to use if the market is above your breakeven and you'd be able to nearly completely eliminate downside price risk.

Let's switch over to corn for this example. Assume the current market is near $3.80. A $3.50 put trades for $0.14 and a $4.40 call trades for $0.17. As before, you'd buy the put and sell the call. Again, assume total fees and commissions are $0.03. Your net cost is $0.14.

To start, here is a chart showing the producer's inherent long position along with the $3.50 put. Notice the minimum price to the producer is $3.36 ($3.50 - $0.14):

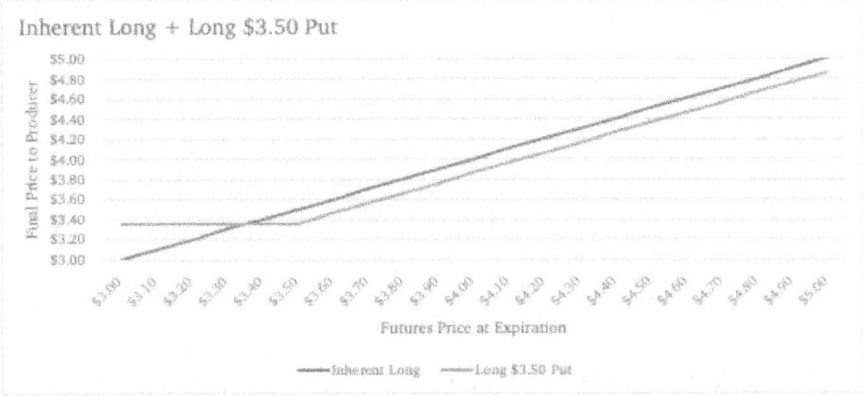

Now the producer's inherent long and short $4.40 call:

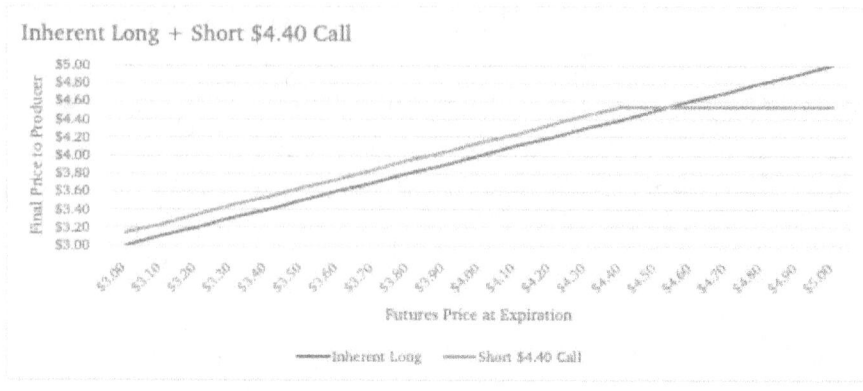

Inherent Long + Short $4.40 Call

And finally, we add them together:

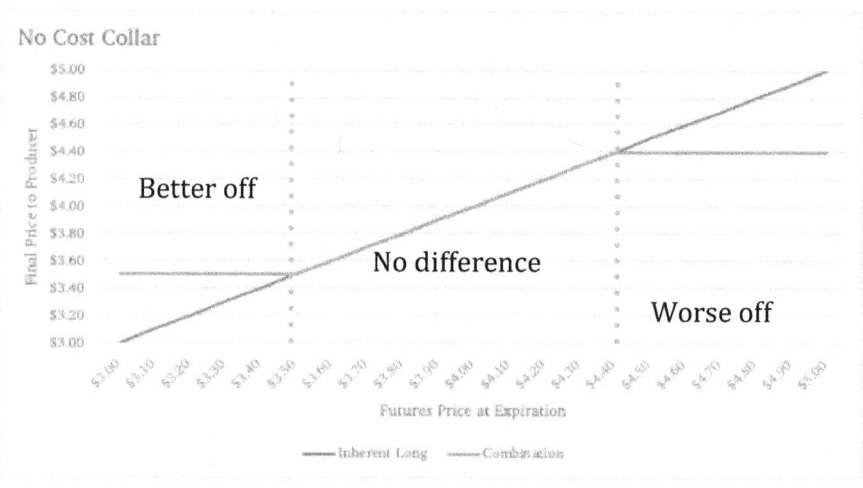

No Cost Collar

The producer has a defined floor at the strike price of the put purchased and a defined ceiling at the strike price of the call sold net less fees and commissions. Because there is no premium cost associated with this position the producer is able to participate in the rally directly with no premium lag, as was the case with the earlier example. Flip back a few pages and notice how the combination strategy yielded a lower price to the producer than the inherent long by the amount of premium paid.

Just to be clear, this chart shows where the producer is better off, the same, and worse off with the option spread:

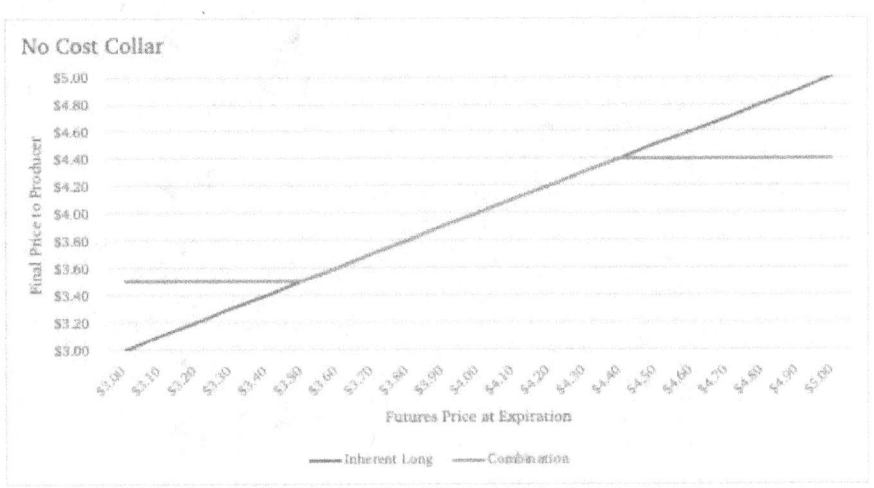

Let's see how this translates to revenue. Our hypothetical producer from the Buying Puts chapter has 500 acres of corn that yields 200 bushels per acre. His cost is $700 per acre. This is what his revenue matrix would look like with no sales and no insurance protection:

	-12.5%	-10.0%	-7.5%	-5.0%	-2.5%	Yield	2.5%	5.0%	7.5%	10.0%	12.5%	15.0%	17.5%
	175	180	185	190	195	200	205	210	215	220	225	230	235
5.1	192.51	218.01	243.51	269.01	294.51	320.01	345.51	371.01	396.51	422.01	447.51	473.01	498.51
5	175.01	200.01	225.01	250.01	275.01	300.01	325.01	350.01	375.01	400.01	425.01	450.01	475.01
4.9	157.51	182.01	206.51	231.01	255.51	280.01	304.51	329.01	353.51	378.01	402.51	427.01	451.51
4.8	140.01	164.01	188.01	212.01	236.01	260.01	284.01	308.01	332.01	356.01	380.01	404.01	428.01
4.7	122.51	146.01	169.51	193.01	216.51	240.01	263.51	287.01	310.51	334.01	357.51	381.01	404.51
4.6	105.01	128.01	151.01	174.01	197.01	220.01	243.01	266.01	289.01	312.01	335.01	358.01	381.01
4.5	87.51	110.01	132.51	155.01	177.51	200.01	222.51	245.01	267.51	290.01	312.51	335.01	357.51
4.4	70.01	92.01	114.01	136.01	158.01	180.01	202.01	224.01	246.01	268.01	290.01	312.01	334.01
4.3	52.51	74.01	95.51	117.01	138.51	160.01	181.51	203.01	224.51	246.01	267.51	289.01	310.51
4.2	35.01	56.01	77.01	98.01	119.01	140.01	161.01	182.01	203.01	224.01	245.01	266.01	287.01
4.1	17.51	38.01	58.51	79.01	99.51	120.01	140.51	161.01	181.51	202.01	222.51	243.01	263.51
4	0.01	20.01	40.01	60.01	80.01	100.01	120.01	140.01	160.01	180.01	200.01	220.01	240.01
3.9	-17.49	2.01	21.51	41.01	60.51	80.01	99.51	119.01	138.51	158.01	177.51	197.01	216.51
3.8	-34.99	-15.99	3.01	22.01	41.01	60.01	79.01	98.01	117.01	136.01	155.01	174.01	193.01
3.7	-52.49	-33.99	-15.49	3.01	21.51	40.01	58.51	77.01	95.51	114.01	132.51	151.01	169.51
3.6	-69.99	-51.99	-33.99	-15.99	2.01	20.01	38.01	56.01	74.01	92.01	110.01	128.01	146.01
3.5	-87.49	-69.99	-52.49	-34.99	-17.49	0.01	17.51	35.01	52.51	70.01	87.51	105.01	122.51
3.4	-104.99	-87.99	-70.99	-53.99	-36.99	-19.99	-2.99	14.01	31.01	48.01	65.01	82.01	99.01
3.3	-122.49	-105.99	-89.49	-72.99	-56.49	-39.99	-23.49	-6.99	9.51	26.01	42.51	59.01	75.51
3.2	-139.99	-123.99	-107.99	-91.99	-75.99	-59.99	-43.99	-27.99	-11.99	4.01	20.01	36.01	52.01
3.1	-157.49	-141.99	-126.49	-110.99	-95.49	-79.99	-64.49	-48.99	-33.49	-17.99	-2.49	13.01	28.51
3	-174.99	-159.99	-144.99	-129.99	-114.99	-99.99	-84.99	-69.99	-54.99	-39.99	-24.99	-9.99	5.01
2.9	-192.49	-177.99	-163.49	-148.99	-134.49	-119.99	-105.49	-90.99	-76.49	-61.99	-47.49	-32.99	-18.49
2.8	-209.99	-195.99	-181.99	-167.99	-153.99	-139.99	-125.99	-111.99	-97.99	-83.99	-69.99	-55.99	-41.99
2.7	-227.49	-213.99	-200.49	-186.99	-173.49	-159.99	-146.49	-132.99	-119.49	-105.99	-92.49	-78.99	-65.49
2.6	-244.99	-231.99	-218.99	-205.99	-192.99	-179.99	-166.99	-153.99	-140.99	-127.99	-114.99	-101.99	-88.99

He obviously has price risk. Further, if the market is currently near $3.80 as stated above, he is making money with his typical yield. By purchasing a $3.50 put he is able to eliminate a majority of his price risk. Adding the short call finances that and builds in a profitable sale at $4.40. This is what his new matrix would look like if this were done on 100% of his crop:

	-12.5%	-10.0%	-7.5%	-5.0%	-2.5%	Yield	2.5%	5.0%	7.5%	10.0%	12.5%	15.0%	17.5%
	175	180	185	190	195	200	205	210	215	220	225	230	235
5.1	52.09	77.59	103.09	128.59	154.09	179.59	205.09	230.59	256.09	281.59	307.09	332.59	358.09
5	54.6	79.6	104.6	129.6	154.6	179.6	204.6	229.6	254.6	279.6	304.6	329.6	354.6
4.9	57.11	81.61	106.11	130.61	155.11	179.61	204.11	228.61	253.11	277.61	302.11	326.61	351.11
4.8	59.62	83.62	107.62	131.62	155.62	179.62	203.62	227.62	251.62	275.62	299.62	323.62	347.62
4.7	62.12	85.62	109.12	132.62	156.12	179.62	203.12	226.62	250.12	273.62	297.12	320.62	344.12
4.6	64.63	87.63	110.63	133.63	156.63	179.63	202.63	225.63	248.63	271.63	294.63	317.63	340.63
4.5	67.14	89.64	112.14	134.64	157.14	179.64	202.14	224.64	247.14	269.64	292.14	314.64	337.14
4.4	69.65	91.65	113.65	135.65	157.65	179.65	201.65	223.65	245.65	267.65	289.65	311.65	333.65
4.3	52.16	73.66	95.16	116.66	138.16	159.66	181.16	202.66	224.16	245.66	267.16	288.66	310.16
4.2	34.66	55.66	76.66	97.66	118.66	139.66	160.66	181.66	202.66	223.66	244.66	265.66	286.66
4.1	17.17	37.67	58.17	78.67	99.17	119.67	140.17	160.67	181.17	201.67	222.17	242.67	263.17
4	-0.32	19.68	39.68	59.68	79.68	99.68	119.68	139.68	159.68	179.68	199.68	219.68	239.68
3.9	-17.81	1.69	21.19	40.69	60.19	79.69	99.19	118.69	138.19	157.69	177.19	196.69	216.19
3.8	-35.3	-16.3	2.7	21.7	40.7	59.7	78.7	97.7	116.7	135.7	154.7	173.7	192.7
3.7	-52.8	-34.3	-15.8	2.7	21.2	39.7	58.2	76.7	95.2	113.7	132.2	150.7	169.2
3.6	-70.29	-52.29	-34.29	-16.29	1.71	19.71	37.71	55.71	73.71	91.71	109.71	127.71	145.71
3.5	-87.78	-70.28	-52.78	-35.28	-17.78	-0.28	17.22	34.72	52.22	69.72	87.22	104.72	122.22
3.4	-85.27	-68.27	-51.27	-34.27	-17.27	-0.27	16.73	33.73	50.73	67.73	84.73	101.73	118.73
3.3	-82.76	-65.26	-49.76	-33.26	-16.76	-0.26	16.24	32.74	49.24	65.74	82.24	98.74	115.24
3.2	-80.26	-64.26	-48.26	-32.26	-16.26	-0.26	15.74	31.74	47.74	63.74	79.74	95.74	111.74
3.1	-77.75	-62.25	-46.75	-31.25	-15.75	-0.25	15.25	30.75	46.25	61.75	77.25	92.75	108.25
3	-75.24	-60.24	-45.24	-30.24	-15.24	-0.24	14.76	29.76	44.76	59.76	74.76	89.76	104.76
2.9	-72.73	-58.23	-43.73	-29.23	-14.73	-0.23	14.27	28.77	43.27	57.77	72.27	86.77	101.27
2.8	-70.22	-56.22	-42.22	-28.22	-14.22	-0.22	13.78	27.78	41.78	55.78	69.78	83.78	97.78
2.7	-67.72	-54.22	-40.72	-27.22	-13.72	-0.22	13.28	26.78	40.28	53.78	67.28	80.78	94.28
2.6	-65.21	-52.21	-39.21	-26.21	-13.21	-0.21	12.79	25.79	38.79	51.79	64.79	77.79	90.79

Quite the improvement. While we did cap profits at a normal yield and below we also were able to reduce his losses to less than a dollar on a move below $3.50. Further, compare the losses on the first matrix on the lower left side to this matrix. It didn't take much of a yield drag and fall in price before to put this producer in a place where he was losing hundreds of dollars an acre. Now the put is able to shoulder the burden of a decline in price.

CHAPTER 7

RATIO SPREADS

Probably the single best trade I ever recommended to my clients was a ratio spread on corn in 2015. I'm not including the following specifics to be braggadocious, I'm including it to illustrate the perfect conditions that were present at the time that led to the recommendation. It's certainly important to remind readers that past performance is not necessarily indicative of future results.

The corn market had rallied in the early part of the summer, and by the time we were close to a peak, it was pretty evident we were going to have a great crop. Without any demand stimulus sustaining the rally was unlikely but not out of the question. You livestock guys know that when a bull wants to run, you get the hell out of the way. We briefly traded to 450'0 December corn, and I recommended buying an at-the-money put (440'0 for most clients) and selling two 500'0 calls to finance this. The timing was perfect, and we paid around a penny and a half for the spread and sold it for about eighty cents a few weeks later. That was a home run of a scale I haven't repeated since.

Now let's look at the mechanics of that trade, the protection it gave, and why on earth I'd sell two calls.

You are probably already familiar with this idea if you sell grain to one of the larger grain companies. It is usually called an "accelerator" contract or something similar. You have a floor under X number of bushels, and if the market rallies to a certain level, you double your commitment. Great for all parties involved.

In my trade from 2015, the reasons for putting a floor under the market at 440'0 (well, 438'4 because we paid a penny and a half for the spread) were pretty obvious at the time. We had finally rallied out of terrible prices and the market looked like it was ready to peak. Selling the two 500'0 calls was a way to force producers to make very profitable sales at a time when euphoria may have taken over if we rallied that far. After all, 2012 and $8+ corn were fresh in our minds. "If we made it to five, we were surely going to six!" would have been the psychology of many.

However, the main reason to sell two calls was so that we could finance nearly 100% of the put. That let us put a floor right under the market price at the time. That's obviously the big benefit to a ratio spread. The risk is having to cough up twice the grain (or dollar equivalent) if the market were to rally to where you sold the calls.

The lesson? Be sure you are okay selling grain at that price. Obvious enough, right? Also be sure you haven't over-committed quantity-wise. By design, you are only able to protect half the quantity you are willing to sell at the higher price. That's what makes these difficult to use early in the year. You are hardly able to protect an appreciable quantity because the risk of a crop failure exists. As summer comes and you have a good idea of your worst-case production this can become one of your go-to strategies.

CHAPTER 8

OPTION PRICING

There are two main determinants of the price of an option. The one you're most familiar with is the intrinsic value, sometimes called the "money-ness." That is, it's the price of the underlying futures contract relative to the strike price of the particular option.

The other main component is time. The more time remaining until expiration, the more the option costs, holding all else equal. Volatility is factored into time value. And finally, the current risk-free interest rate. This last piece hasn't been much of a factor in recent times, but is worth mentioning even though I won't cover it in detail here.

Intrinsic Value

As you read in the Basic Definitions chapter under "strike price," the moneyness, or intrinsic value, is the difference between the strike price and the price of the underlying futures contract. An option can be "in the money," "at the money," or "out of the money." In the case of put options, the put is in the money if the futures price is below the strike price.

Example: A $4.50 corn put is in the money if the underlying futures are less than $4.50.

The importance of this factor is most obvious when the option expires. If there is no intrinsic value at that time the option is worthless. Stated another way, at expiration the only value of an option is its intrinsic value.

Consider this chart that shows the intrinsic value of a $4.00 corn put:

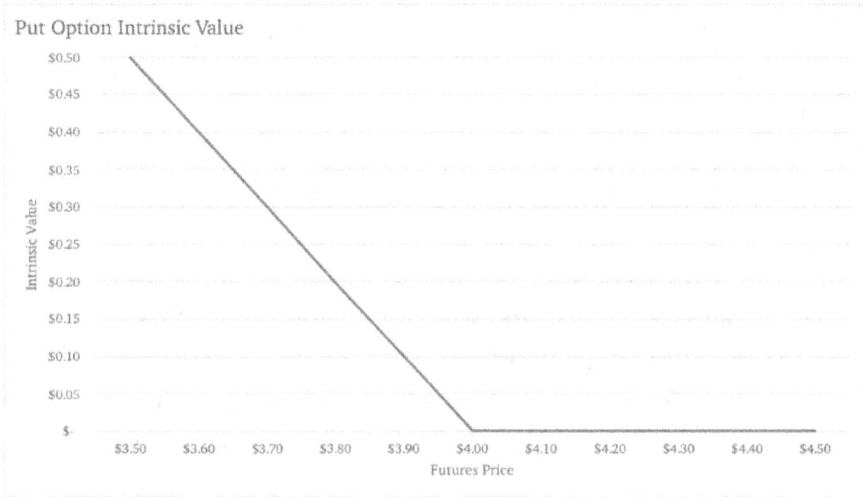

At $4.00 and above there is no intrinsic value. At every price below $4.00 the intrinsic value is equal to $4.00 minus the futures price.

Strike Price	-	Futures Price	=	Intrinsic Value
$4.00	-	$4.00	=	0
$4.00	-	$3.90	=	0.10
$4.00	-	$3.80	=	0.20
$4.00	-	$3.70	=	0.30
4.00	-	3.60	=	0.40

Time Value

At this point you may wonder why options still have value if they aren't in the money. Time value or time premium answers that question. This is the portion of an option's premium that is made up of the value of the time remaining until the option expires. Because the moneyness is known as the intrinsic value this can be thought of as the extrinsic value of an option. Simply put:

Option price – Intrinsic value = Time value

The time premium shrinks as time goes on. This is known as "time decay." An option loses about one third of its time premium in the first half of its life and the rest in the second half. Time decay accelerates as expiration approaches (generally falling fastest in the last thirty days before expiration).

Let's look at time value graphically by plotting the value of a $4.00 corn put. This is similar to the previous chart except the vertical axis is now "option price" rather than "intrinsic value." The flat line represents the price of the option at expiration, which we know is just the intrinsic value. The curved line represents the price of the option with a few months of time left before it expires.

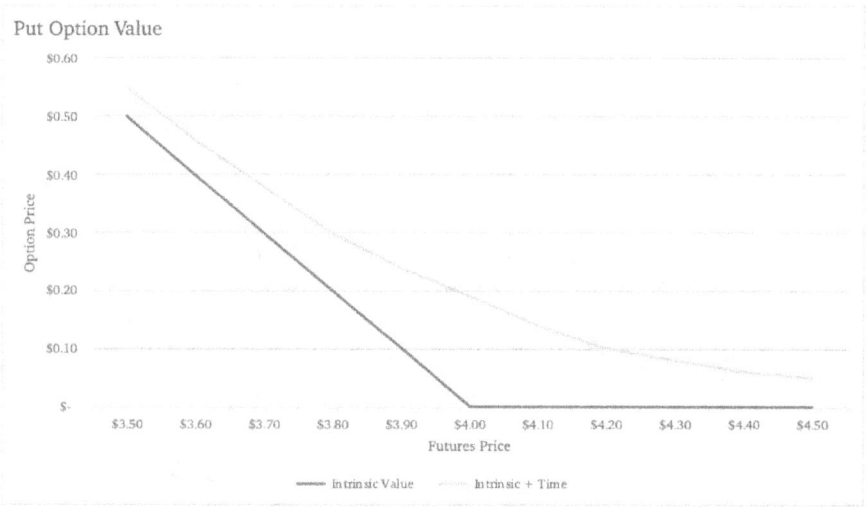

Put Option Value

Intrinsic Value   Intrinsic + Time

This illustrates the earlier formula that states that time value is equal to the price of the option less time value. You can look at time value on the chart as the difference between the two lines. Notice how it is widest at the strike price ($4.00). This is so because when an option is at the money its opportunity to gain intrinsic value is at its greatest.

Another way to think about that concept is to think that time value is someone paying for uncertainty. The more uncertainty the higher the price commanded. If an option is very far in the money or out of the money you become more certain it will either expire with great intrinsic value or worthless. But an at the money option could go either way.

Of course, as time goes on the chances of an option expiring in the money decrease. There are simply fewer opportunities for price to move.

This chart that shows what the value of an option might be from as time goes on. We start with the now familiar intrinsic value line, followed by a line that shows the price of the put with three months to expiration, along with lines for six months, and nine months to show the contrast.

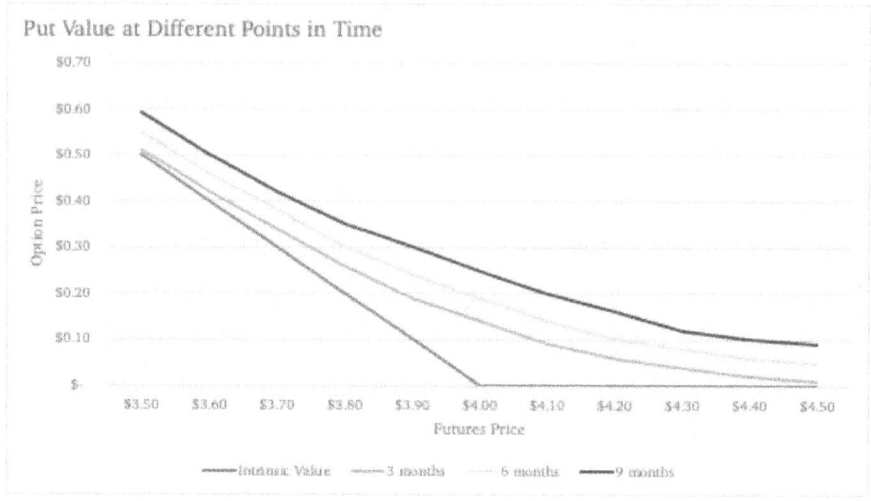

Put Value at Different Points in Time

Here's another way to look at this concept. The chart on the next page shows the percent of the total value of a $10.00 soybean put at different times before expiration/

With 156 days until expiration the intrinsic value of the option is only 8% while the time value is 92% We know that at expiration there is no time value whatsoever. A little more than halfway between the 156-day mark and expiration we have 65 days. You can see that time value still makes up an overwhelming majority of the option's value. Only with a few days left does the intrinsic value become the driver of the premium. This illustrates the concept of time decay.

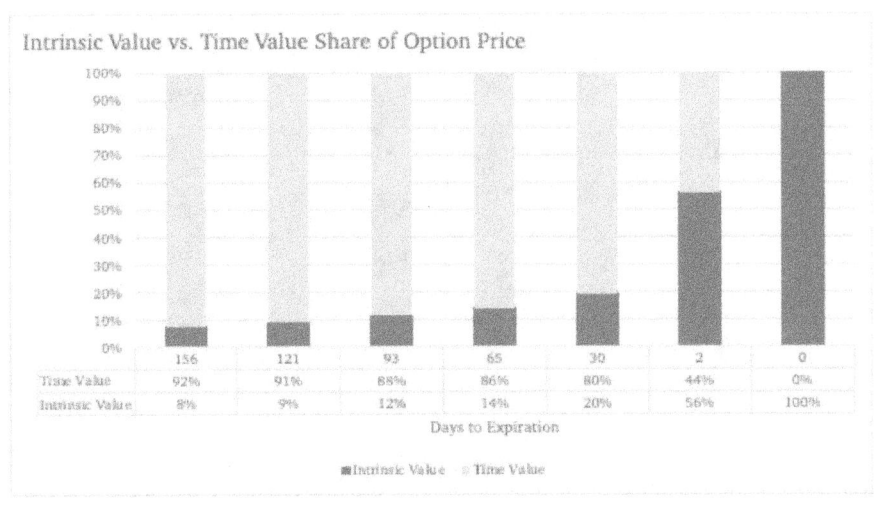

Intrinsic Value vs. Time Value Share of Option Price

	156	121	93	65	30	2	0
Time Value	92%	91%	88%	86%	80%	44%	0%
Intrinsic Value	8%	9%	12%	14%	20%	56%	100%

Days to Expiration

■ Intrinsic Value   ▫ Time Value

Time Decay

Options are wasting assets. That means, as you've seen, that as time goes on, they lose value. The rate at which this time value is eroded is known as "theta." We don't need to dive deep into the option Greeks, as they're called. But the concept is illustrated by the following example:

An $10.00 soybean put costs $0.50. It has a theta of -.10. Thus, it will experience a drop in price, holding all else equal, of $0.05 per day. So in a week (five trading days) the price of the option will fall from $0.50 to $0.25.

As expiration nears theta increases, or the time value decays faster as we near expiration.

Consider the following chart that shows the time value of a $10.00 soybean put. Notice how time value falls more rapidly as the days to expiration approaches zero.

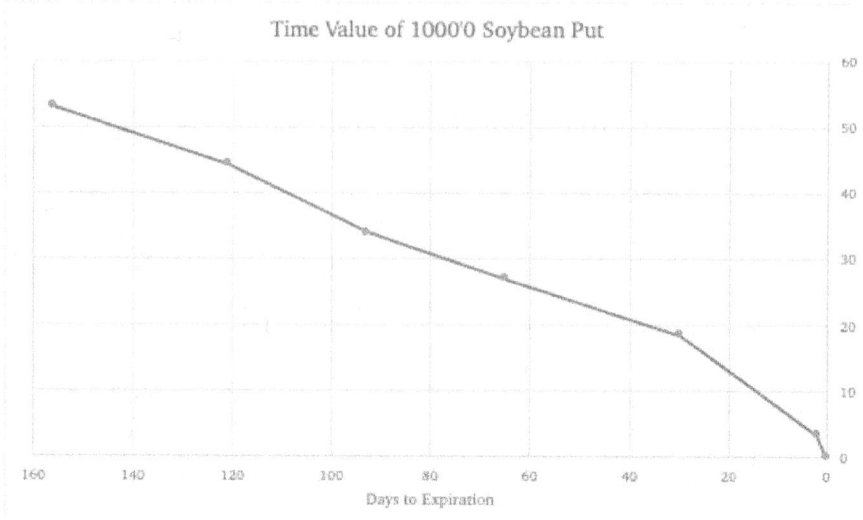

Time Value of 1000'0 Soybean Put

A fun (if you're weird like me) fact is the rate of decay is related to the square root of how much time remains before expiration. An option with three months remaining loses time premium twice as fast as one with nine months to go (square root of 9 = 3). An option with two months remaining loses time premium twice as fast as one with four months (square root of 4 = 2), and so on.

CHAPTER 9

VOLATILITY

"Historical volatility measures volatility looking back, while implied volatility measures expectations going forward."

In my opinion volatility is the most overlooked and misunderstood aspect of using options as an instrument to manage risk for farmers. Simply, volatility is a measure of how much the underlying futures contract moves and to what magnitude. For me, it is the single most important aspect of option trading.

As we learned, volatility is a major determinant of the price of an option. Holding all else equal, if volatility increases the price an option will increase as well. Conversely, a decline in volatility will cause an option to depreciate.

So, what does volatility look like? Here is a chart showing two hypothetical price paths for a commodity that start and end in the same place:

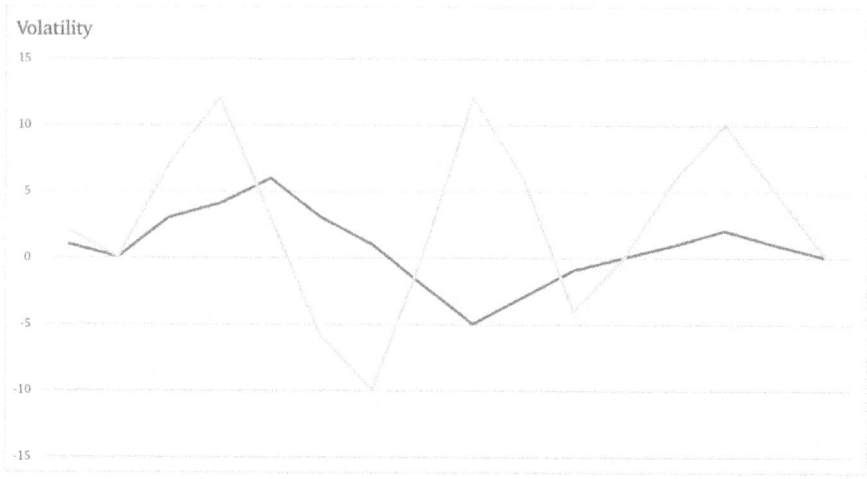

Without analyzing it much it is quite obvious that one line is much more erratic than the other. Accordingly, it is the more volatile price path. For a hedger that would likely mean the options on that contract are going to be relatively more expensive than options on the other path.

Why then does higher volatility equal higher option premiums? The answer is because when volatility is high the market can have a wider distribution in price. That means an option would have better odds of finishing in the money, so option writers need to be compensated for that risk. On the flip side, if an option is more likely to be in the money an option buyer would likely be willing to pay more to assume the enhanced odds of taking assignment in the underlying futures contract.

There are generally two ways analysts assess volatility: historical volatility and implied volatility. Historical volatility measures volatility looking back, while implied volatility measures expectations going forward.

Historical Volatility

Let's start by defining historical volatility. Mathematically it is simply the annualized standard deviation of the daily changes in the underlying futures contract.

Take a look at the following table that shows the price of corn for the previous fifteen days for both a high volatility year and a low volatility year. These, by the way, are the same prices used in the chart example earlier in this chapter showing the two price paths with differing volatilities.

While the math isn't terribly important to understand, as a hedger working with a broker who has experience trading volatility, I always like to make sure my clients have an understanding of the theories and strategies I suggest. For that reason, we'll take a moment here to work through the math.

First, historical volatility has what's known as a "look-back period." That is basically how many days you are analyzing to come up with the historical volatility number for the next day in the series. In this instance we are using a look-back period of fifteen days.

Once you have the settlement prices for the look-back period the next step is calculating the percentage change in price from day to day. From those figures you would compute the standard deviation of the changes. A spreadsheet program will do the hard work for you. If you are using Microsoft Excel the formula is:

=stdev.p(look-back period percentage changes)

	High Volatility		Low Volatility	
	Price	% Change	Price	% Change
Day 1	$4.50		$4.50	
Day 2	$4.65	3.33%	$4.53	0.67%
Day 3	$4.72	1.51%	$4.48	-1.10%
Day 4	$4.63	-1.91%	$4.39	-2.01%
Day 5	$4.50	-2.81%	$4.41	0.46%
Day 6	$4.37	-2.89%	$4.47	1.36%
Day 7	$4.50	2.97%	$4.51	0.89%
Day 8	$4.61	2.44%	$4.60	2.00%
Day 9	$4.80	4.12%	$4.63	0.65%
Day 10	$4.95	3.13%	$4.64	0.22%
Day 11	$4.72	-4.65%	$4.70	1.29%
Day 12	$4.60	-2.54%	$4.72	0.43%
Day 13	$4.41	-4.13%	$4.68	-0.85%
Day 14	$4.25	-3.63%	$4.60	-1.71%
Day 15	$4.53	6.59%	$4.53	-1.52%
Standard Deviation	3.55%			1.22%
Square Root (252)	15.87			15.87
Historical Volatility	56%			19%

Recall that historical volatility is the *annualized* standard deviation. That means we now need to figure out how to annualize the data. The way to do that is to take the square root of the number of trading days in a year (usually 252). In Excel:

=sqrt(252)

Finally, the historical volatility is just the standard deviation you computed multiplied by the square root of 252.

Here's the bottom part of that table again:

Standard Deviation	3.55%		1.22%
Square Root (252)	15.87		15.87
Historical Volatility	56%		19%

When expressed as a percentage the historical volatility from the price path on the left is significantly higher than that on the right. As a result, you can bet the options for that set on the left will be quite a bit more expensive than the right.

Implied Volatility

Implied volatility is a forward-looking measure of volatility, and represents the expected movement of the underlying futures contract over a specific period of time. The math is pretty similar to historical volatility, so I won't cover it again, but there is one key difference. Historical volatility, as you recall, is a measure of the annualized standard deviation of the underlying contract. Implied volatility is the annualized *expected* standard deviation.

The distinction may seem small, but it's really quite important. It is what provides the basis for identifying potentially mispriced options. If implied volatility is significantly higher or lower than the historical average, it could be actionable.

Seasonal Volatility

Let's briefly look at seasonal volatility now. When you think of all the things that can be thrown at a crop and make or break price what is the number one thing? Risks during the growing season, right? Like a cornered animal the grain markets have a tendency to be more volatile when they are most at risk. And of course, the crops are most at risk during critical periods of the summer when concerns about heat and moisture are at the forefront of everyone's mind.

Therefore, options are most often *relatively* more expensive during the summer months.

Volatility in the corn market tends to peak as pollination weather becomes known during the end of June through the middle part of July, and soybean volatility tends to peak in late July.

Here are some charts showing the average of past years' historical volatility:

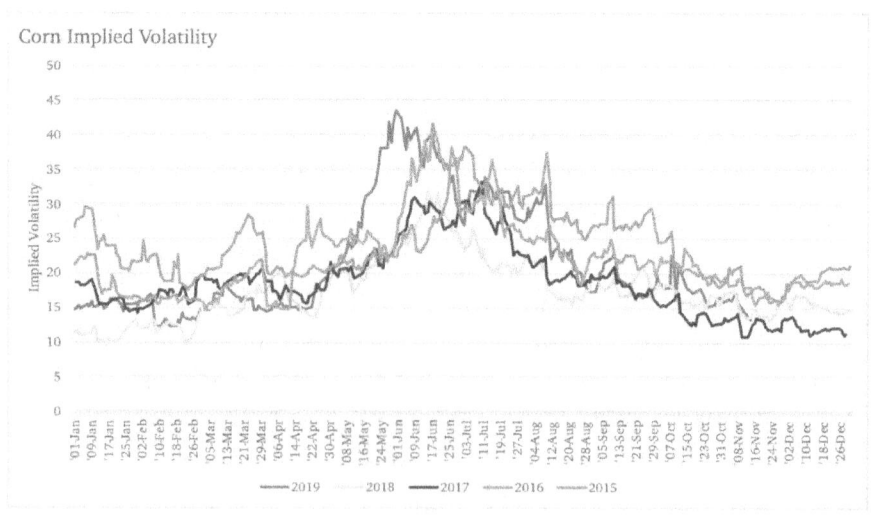

Corn Average Implied Volatility 2015-2019

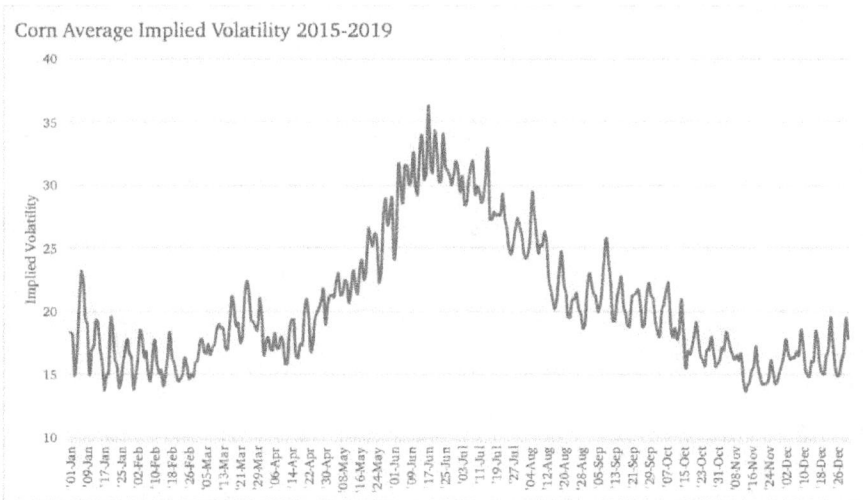

Soybean Implied Volatility

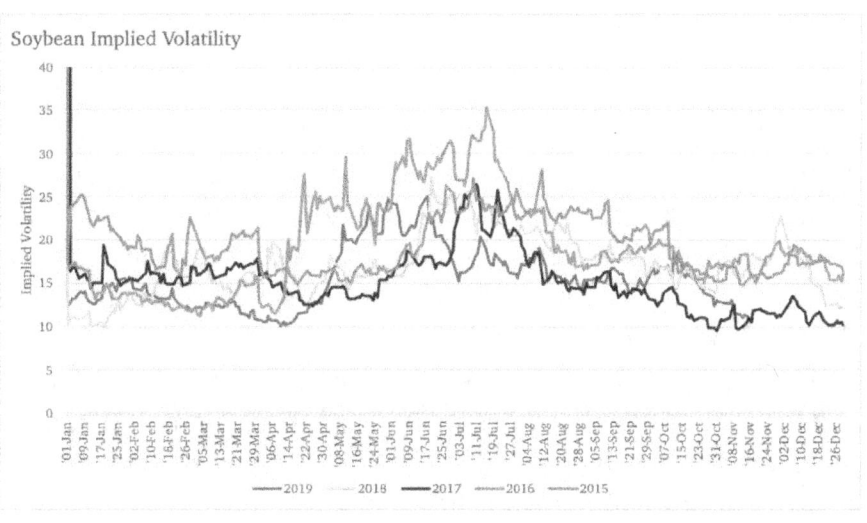

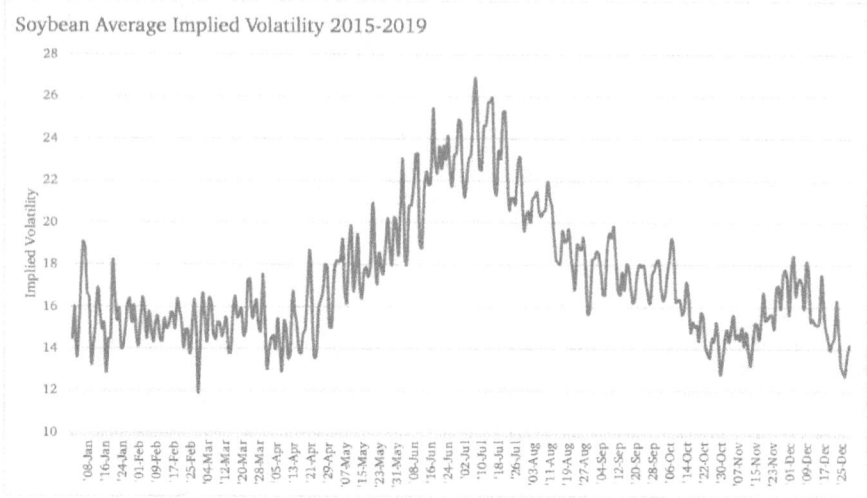

Soybean Average Implied Volatility 2015-2019

Date source: Refinitiv

What does all this mean for you as a grain producer? Well, holding all else equal when volatility is high you generally want to be a seller of options; when volatility is low you want to be a buyer of them. Now, selling options by themselves can be very risky business and inherently has more risks than buying them. This is also known as selling them "naked."

If selling (writing) options alone isn't in the cards for you and/or you are more interested in protecting current prices you may consider a bear put spread. I'll detail that type of strategy later on along with the others.

I really think that once you start tracking volatility on your own using either a spreadsheet or charting package (most include historical volatility as an indicator) you will have a much better understanding of how options are priced and when to employ the various strategies.

CHAPTER 10

WHEN TO ROLL OPTIONS

One of the most commonly questioned techniques with option hedging is rolling them up or down. By and large, grain producers will be rolling put options. There are two reasons to do this. The first is the market is rallying and it has moved above your strike price. In this instance your option is losing value but the rise in the market is making up for it. The second scenario is the market is falling and your put is growing further and further in the money.

Rolling puts up

Say for example you purchased a 1000'0 soybean put at 30'0. You level you were protecting was 970'0 (1000'0-30'0). Unexpected bullish news comes into the market and it rallies up to 1030'0. While your physical soybeans are worth thirty cents more per bushel your option is now only worth 10'0. It seems silly to maintain a 970'0 floor when the market is a full sixty cents better. You don't want to lock in a price yet but still wish to maintain protection. Now we have some math to do.

Assume as well that a 1030'0 put is now trading for 30'0. Does it make sense to replace your 1000'0 put with the 1030'0?

Here's how to work the math:

Old floor:
Original strike – original premium = old floor
1000'0 – 30'0 = 970'0

Loss on original put:
Premium originally paid – current premium
30'0 – 10'0 = 20'0

New floor:
New strike – new premium – loss on original put
1030'0 – 30'0 – 20'0 = 980'0

Even with the loss of premium, we are able to roll the option up and raise our floor ten cents. Here's one thing I hear a lot from clients: "well, it's only a dime. It's hardly worth it." Bull. As long as you are still in need of put protection and the difference is greater than your transaction costs, you should probably roll the put up. Do the math on the bushels you are protecting. 500 acres at 50 bushels per acre is a 25,000 bushel crop. Only a dime is $2,500. If you saw a $50 bill sitting on the sidewalk, you wouldn't hesitate to pick it up, would you? Why not pick up a higher floor if the market is offering it?

Rolling puts down

The other side of this is if your puts are now in the money and you are worried about protecting the profit in the trade. It's important to always think of options as a hedging vehicle rather than a trading vehicle. However, options that aren't managed have a tendency to become worthless. The idea behind rolling a put down is taking profit on your original position, putting the money back in your pocket, and purchasing a put with a lower strike price at the money.

Assume you purchased a 1000'0 put for 30'0 when the market was trading at 1000'0. Let's say the price of soybeans is now 900'0 and your option is worth 120'0. 900'0 puts are trading at 20'0.

The math is easy when it comes to your price floor. Your original floor, just like in the earlier example, is 970'0: seventy cents higher than where the market is now! At the same time, you have ninety cents of profit in that (120'0 – 30'0) and you don't want to lose it. Where does that put your new floor if you were to book the profit?

New floor:
New strike – new premium + profit on old put
900'0 – 20'0 + 90'0 = 970'0

A bit of a curveball, isn't it? In this example our floor stays the same. So why would you roll the put down? Well, you felt the market had the potential to rise from the current level you have the profit from the original put to add on to wherever you sell. That ninety cents isn't going anywhere once you roll the put down. Consider as well that you are spending money on the new put and that takes away from what you can add on to your cash sale. At the end of the day you are tacking seventy cents onto wherever you end up pricing the beans.

The usefulness of this is especially evident if the market is somewhere between the old and new put at expiration. Say it is below your original floor but not by much. 950'0 for example. Well, 950'0 + 70'0 (your profit) is 1020'0. That's a better price than you were originally protecting.

These may be idealized examples with hypothetical prices, but the math is the same. You can do the math on the back of a napkin and determine if it is worth doing.

ABOUT THE AUTHOR

Jeff works one-on-one with commodity producers, users, and individual speculators and focuses on grain and livestock markets. He has presented live and online seminars sponsored by CME Group, written for Stocks and Commodities Magazine, and has been quoted in Barrons, Reuters, The Wall Street Journal, Successful Farming, and many others. Jeff graduated from Northern Illinois University where he majored in Economics.

Jeff is the President and CEO of Kapco Futures, Inc., a brokerage firm that specializes in creating advanced risk management strategies for commodity producers and end-users. He is also the CEO of Cattle Core, LLC, a livestock risk management software company.